BLACK ENOUGH/
WHITE ENOUGH

BLACK ENOUGH/
WHITE ENOUGH
THE OBAMA DILEMMA

By Rickey Hendon
Foreword by Hermene D. Hartman

Progressive Black Publishing Since 1967

Third World Press
Chicago

Third World Press
Publishers since 1967
Chicago

First Edition
Printed in the United States of America

Cover Design: Sirita Render

Library of Congress Cataloging-in-Publication Data

Hendon, Rickey, 1953-
  Black enough/White enough : the Obama dilemma/by Rickey Hendon with David Smallwood; foreword by Hermene D. Hartman. — 1st ed.
      p. cm.
  Includes bibliographical references and index.
  ISBN-13: 978-0-88378-309-2 (pbk.)
  ISBN-10: 0-88378-309-6 (pbk.)
  1. Obama, Barack. 2. Obama, Barack—Political and social views. 3. Presidential candidates—United States—Biography. 4. Presidents—United States—Election—2008. 5. Political campaigns—United States—History—21st century. 6. African American legislators—United States—Biography. 7. African American legislators—Illinois—Biography. 8. Racially mixed people—Race identity—United States. 9. United States—Race relations—Political aspects. 10. Hendon, Rickey, 1953- I. Smallwood, David. II. Title.
  E901.1.O23H46 2009
  973.932092—dc22

[B]
                              2008048659

13 12 11 10 09   6 5 4 3 2 1

I dedicate this book to my mother, Olivia, and my father, Jimmy. May their memories live forever.

I acknowledge almighty God for giving me the gift of self-expression and the nerve to share this gift with others for the good of mankind.

I want to thank my family for bearing with me while I put the book first. I love all of you, I really do—I just had to concentrate!

I want to offer a special thanks to the most positively persistent woman in the world, *N'DIGO* publisher Hermene Hartman, who told me I have talent and I must write this book for the sake of history and for my own mental well being.

I could never forget David Smallwood for his patience and understanding of my work and the way he pulled my thoughts and observations together.

I also want to thank all of the fine people who elected me and put me in a position to know such a great man, Barack Obama. Your confidence in me has not been misplaced.

Finally, I want to thank the wonderful people at Third World Press. From the moment Hermene and I walked through their door, I knew I was at home.

CONTENTS

Two Gentlemen From Illinois: A Perspective
By Hermene D. Hartman

The 2008 presidential race to the White House will go down in history in more ways than one. Over the past two years there has been any number of upsets and surprises in this historic race. New faces have appeared, old faces have vanished, and a new history has been born.

New media mastery and image perception have dominated more than real issues and political substance, and this opinionated drama has featured all of the "isms"—to put it politely, the issues of the pursuit have been racism, sexism, and ageism—front row and center. The candidates may have alluded to, but not directly addressed them, indeed, it has been the chatter by the voters at the cocktail party, in the beauty shop, and at the water cooler. The Democratic primary was a contest of sexism and racism as much as it was a race among candidates. The issues there were: Is America ready for a Black president? Is America ready for a woman president? Who goes first?

We have witnessed Barack Obama go and grow from the State Capitol of Illinois, Springfield, home of the greatest president in our history, Abraham Lincoln, and the site where Obama chose to make his announcement to run—to engaging in the ridiculous lipstick politics of Sarah Palin, as Republican vice presidential candidate.

From my front row seat of watching Barack Obama, his political rise has been astonishing. I first met Barack after he authored his book, *Dreams Of My Father*. In August of 1995, Barack wrote me a letter of introduction at the suggestion of a mutual friend, Kaye Wilson. At the time, he was a young lawyer full of promise and determination and had the fire in his belly to be a public servant. He wanted an article about his book in *N'DIGO*, the popular magapaper that I publish in Chicago. He was a great promoter—persistent, and alone, there were no public relations people.

My initial impression was that he was the ultimate professional—a beautiful writer, engaging, and that he saw the political scene slightly differently. I was interested in his political career and I have watched Barack progress into a political powerhouse.

I lived in Hyde Park, a district that he came to represent as an Illinois state senator and I supported his candidacy. Barack followed in the footsteps of an identity known in Chicago as the liberal politician who was more concerned with being on the right side of issues and raising proper questions than Chicago's rough and tough political landscape.

He followed the footsteps of legendary Chicago elected officials like Leon Despres, Adlai Stevenson, Paul Simon, Richard Newhouse, and Paul Douglas. Barack was the perfect gentleman to represent Hyde Park's intellectual, urban-mixed, university community.

A very good friend of Barack Obama's is Jim Reynolds, founder of Loop Markets, LLC, the largest Black-owned investment firm in the country, which is located in Chicago. Jim was also president of a Black business consortium in the city called the Alliance of Business Leaders and Entrepreneurs (ABLE), to which I also belong. Jim introduced Barack to major players in Chicago's business community and also to the Rev. Jesse Jackson. The individuals in this group made up Barack's initial fundraisers for his United States Senate race.

He first came to our attention when he sat in on some of our ABLE meetings to learn first-hand the problems, issues and concerns of small business people. At the meetings Barack was usually quiet and observant, and I was impressed that he was a great listener. Often our discussions revolved around the limitations of the "minority status" reserved for Black business people—that is, the set aside programs that are at best entry-level opportunities, but do not necessarily allow for business maturity. As a business grows, the percentage and market share also needs to grow.

In the meantime, Rev. Jackson invited Barack to his Operation Rainbow/PUSH meetings often on Saturdays to expose him to his crowd and a TV audience.

In many of the ABLE meetings, we all talked about a new model of politics and business. Those early conversations, I think, lead to the reality of Obama's national model with the most important idea being to cross over.

Black firms and Blacks politicians have historically represented their people exclusively, which is a segregated practice. Many fortunes have been made by Black entrepreneurs serving this private ethnic sector, especially in the hair care, cosmetics and magazine industries. But don't whites read magazines, too? Don't whites eat barbecue, too? So, it is also the same principle for the politician. Truly, if we limit ourselves, we hit a ceiling. But should we appeal to the white sector in addition, we cross over and become progressive and have a greater consumer base. We add Hispanics, Asians, and everyone else to that mix, too.

This was a core discussion with what I now refer to as Barack's "day one" people. This is a thinking that was turning the corner among progressive, successful, and highly-educated business people. Why should Barack have to run as a Black politician, or a Black candidate? He has to be a candidate for all. In simple terms, it was necessary that he get a diverse constituency. He had to be the essence of the American candidate, and Barack positioned himself perfectly.

This became a trademark and a real breakthrough for his candidacy. I was part of Rev. Jesse Jackson's presidential campaign in 1988 and have become a student (maybe a scholar) on how the media receives, perceives, and/or rejects the Black candidate. The question is, how Black can you be and how white must you be to be accepted by the masses.

I followed Jim Reynolds as president of ABLE and became the first woman to serve in that position. I was also the first ABLE president to serve a double term, often finding myself in a controversial role because I dared to go beyond our comfort level. ABLE stayed in contact with Barack as his political career advanced. We all wanted to grow beyond our Black societal confines, and this was our common bond. We met with Barack on a regular basis, about every six months, and agreed to be a sounding board for him. We also supported him individually to various degrees.

Jim Reynolds asked me if I would do a cover story on Barack in *N'DIGO* as he ran in the U.S. Senate race. At the time, he was definitely the underdog in the contest that pitted him against two wealthy white candidates, Blair Hull on the Democratic side and Jack Ryan on the Republican. Barack had all of the determination in the world and was confident he could win. We agreed to key principles and we did supportive things to assist his candidacy. He was amazing as he played Illinois and Chicago politics brilliantly, but a step above and beyond.

Barack appeared on the cover of N'DIGO on March 3, 2003, and we were the first publication to give him that kind of media treatment. I had introduced other politicians to the Chicago public through our pages, but Barack was different, and I knew it.

He also appeared frequently as a guest or a guest host on Chicago's Black talk radio station, WVON, owned by my dear friend Melody Spann Cooper. These initial platforms introduced him, and this is where we first read about and heard the voice and politics of Barack Obama. He was honing his political craft and he was listening to the people.

I purchased Savoy magazine in June of 2005 and in February of 2006, Barack and Michelle Obama appeared on our debut cover in a glamour shot as a new Camelot couple. The photo was taken by world acclaimed photographer Victor Skrebneski, and I was mindful to establish an image and a crossover look and feel. I wanted to talk to the Obamas before they went to Washington, and we met on a cold day in early November.

Chris Benson wrote what I still consider to be one of the best stories on Barack. Internally, the editor, Monroe Anderson, and I had lengthy and heated discussions about this cover. It was a relaunch of Savoy, which had gone dormant under the previous owners, and a top entertainer would be more effective on the cover, some thinking went. But I maintained that Barack would go farther, and I wanted to reach farther with the magazine's position. Entertainers come and go. Barack was important, and I wanted an historic cover in more ways than one.

In the meantime, I had become friends with Illinois State Senator Rickey Hendon, who is also my senator, representing the West Loop district where my business office is located just blocks away from Oprah Winfrey's studio. I have always been impressed with Hendon's ability to get things done. He is results-oriented and sometimes uses a hammer approach, but truly is one of the best, most effective politicians I know.

He is a quick wit, a definite fighter, a master at the Chicago game of politics, and the majority whip in the Illinois Senate. Rickey and Barack were both mentored by the Honorable Emil Jones, the President of the Illinois State Senate who single-handedly put the power bounce into Barack's career.

The story goes that Barack had a conversation with Senator Jones, to the point that Jones had the power to make someone a United States Senator. Jones asked whom that someone should be. Barack identified himself as the choice, and a national career began. Chicago politicians take a lot of insults about their questionable doings, but it is an art form to see the pros work. I am certain that Barack benefits from his local politics in Chicago and Illinois, and these lessons have served him well as he rose to the national stage.

Jones determined that Barack would be senator and made everyone line up. He did it with sheer power, force, political astuteness, arm-twisting, confidence, arguments, speeches, and persuasion; Chicago-style politics went into full effect.

There was a meeting held with a Black men's professional organization, The Frogs, whose purpose is to be sociable among their peers and discuss current events. The meeting was attended by the late John Stroger and Emil Jones. Both were long-time political players in the city, county, and state politics as staunch Democrats. They were the chieftains, ruling members of the powerful democratic machine. Stroger was the President of the Cook County Board. Emil was the President of the Senate. Both worked under the tutelage of the Democratic Party Machine.

Both men addressed The Frogs for their support of the U S. Senate candidates. Jones advocated for Barack. Stroger advocated for Dan Hynes, who would become the Comptroller of Illinois, and was the son of Thomas Hynes, a former Chicago political power. Stroger explained his friendship and loyalty to the Hynes family and stated he would have the party support and the funds to win the race. Emil gave a passionate speech on supporting Barack. In part, he said that Barack Obama was everything we could hope for. He was brilliant, educated and a dedicated public servant.

Then he asked the question: at one point, do we support our very own, because he is our own? He asked when do we become loyal to each other. He asked when do we rightfully walk through the door of opportunity for ourselves. He asked when does our democratic loyalty pay off. He asked when do we assert our power for ourselves. He said Barack could be the senator, and all we have to do is support him.

When Emil sat down, some of the men in the room had tears in their eyes and all knew this wasn't politics as usual. Jones impacted the room and the contrast had been old politics versus new politics. The Jones question was, if not now, when? And, if not Barack, then who? Emil Jones became a statesman that evening.

The Frog's meeting was private and secret. I got four late night and early morning calls to discuss the dynamic discussion of the meeting. They all suggested that I must write about it, but couldn't divulge sources. I was sworn to secrecy, but this argument had to be presented publicly. So, I wrote a parable about two elephants and a young lion. One elephant knew he was an elephant. He was a confident powerhouse that could sway and could raise others to new heights with his swagger. He was proud and liked the idea of new talent. He knew he was a mentor.

The other elephant didn't realize he was an elephant—he was a blind loyalist who was an obedient follower. The elephants challenged each other. In the parable, I made Barack the young lion.

That article caused a buzz, and Emil Jones, President of the Illinois Senate, and the only Black man in the country to hold that position at a state level, carried the article in his pocket for a long time. There were many discussions about the elephants, but everyone knew who the lion was. And the smart ones figured out the elephants.

As Barack Obama announced his candidacy for the Democratic Party nomination for President of the United States, Rickey Hendon and I talked regularly, realizing we were watching history in the making. I was writing articles weekly and discussing viewpoints. Rickey was present at the major events. We were students of all news. Hendon used his political resources to support Barack. He assigned his workers and he raised money. He was working it. He was watching television reports and listening to the pundits and he was commenting on what he saw.

We were talking and he was suggesting what I should write as a weekly column. We discussed perspectives and viewpoints. I suggested to Rickey that he begin to keep a journal since his assessments and analysis were so sharp. Your insight is critical, my friend, I told him—it's too bad Barack couldn't hear these conversations first hand.

Rickey served in the Illinois State Senate with Barack and had a unique view of him. He has witnessed Barack's growth and development from a greenhorn to a national powerhouse.

The media began to call Rickey asking for comment. He would call me to ask if he should talk. I began to get calls from national media and international media and *N'DIGO* stories were appearing on the Internet.

Rickey, I said, you need to write a book. Rickey suggested we write the book together—the point being that even as the newly known Black political strategists, pundits, and analysts came forth, there was still an absence of certain voices in the national political discussion.

The conversations between Rickey and me centered a great deal on race and political position and reason. A frequent question was asked, "Is Barack Black enough?" What was behind the question? Isn't it obvious? What philosophy should he have? What did he have to prove? Who did he have to prove it to? Would his mixed heritage be an advantage or a hindrance?

My initial concern was how would Obama be received in the Deep South, by Blacks and whites. I recall that my mother overheard one of our conversations. She commented that mulattos traditionally do well. The thing she said about Barack is that he is mulatto, but didn't come out light skinned with curly hair.

When Barack won the primary in Iowa, clearly he proved he was capable of getting the white vote and that his message of "change" had resonated. He had positioned himself flawlessly. He was raising money at record rates using technology as a non-traditional source.

Barack had cornered the concept of change. He did not present himself as a Black man. He presented a new American, perhaps a new breed with wholesome America intentions and values. He represented a new politician, in Kennedy style. I often reflected on the *Savoy* cover that I argued with so many about. They got it. The young senator, his beautiful wife, glamorized just enough, on the way to the White House.

His speech at the Democratic National Convention in 2004 spoke of one America—not a white America, not a Black America, not a

Hispanic America—but one United States of America. His fresh face and new voice had been heard and would four years later return him back to this national stage.

Barack's leadership was defined. He did not speak about the injustices and America's racist shame. He spoke to promise and opportunity. His was the future. He spoke to what America could be if it would live up to its creed. His rhetoric had enough romance language in it and his dialogue had enough idealism in it to have mass appeal. Young white Americans came running. The world was his oyster. He was the American Dream coming alive. I thought his statement, "You are the one you've been waiting for," said it all. It was spiritual.

Then Rev. Jeremiah Wright appeared in full force. He was taken out of context and a sound bite defined a scholarly minister unfairly. The news sound bite was used repeatedly to remind us that Barack was a Black man through his militant minister, whom he eventually had to dismiss to save his campaign. *Fox News'* Bill O'Reilly had dominated, determined, and directed the political question of the day surrounding Rev. Wright. I appeared on his show to defend and discuss the political dilemma of Barack Obama. I explained that Rev. Wright had been taken out of context. I explained the Black church style, particularly its liberation doctrine.

I even invited O'Reilly to attend Rev. Wright's Trinity Church so that he could see a full service. This never panned out, even though he agreed on air to attend. I was planning a Chicago tour of the Black community for him. I regret that this visit never happened because a first-hand perspective might have changed the topic of this piece of news, which O'Reilly was definitely in control of.

Rickey said Barack was forced to make a hard political decision regarding Wright and that he made the right one. I thought this whole situation could have been media managed better. My final assessment was that the minister's pulpit does not necessarily transfer to a national media stage.

The question of Black enough, white enough was fully engaged with the Wright incident. This was, beyond a doubt was the Obama dilemma. Would he dismiss his minister? This is not something easily done. Is he white enough, will he be smart enough to dismiss him? These were pertinent questions.

After Rev. Wright's session at the National Press Club, there was no hesitation about what had to be done. Black and white didn't have a damn thing to do with it. The campaign was being undermined.

Barack won the Democratic nomination for president. One of the proudest moments ever for Black America was in Denver on August 28, 2008. In 1963, Dr. Martin Luther King Jr. spoke to the nation. In 1988, Jesse Jackson changed the rules of the party and spoke at the convention. In 2008, Barack took the nomination. The veteran civil rights community had been largely ignored by the campaign and none of them appeared on the Democratic National Convention stage, but Barack's acceptance speech was given 45 years to the day after Dr. King's March on Washington "I Have a Dream" speech. Barack, however, did not call Dr. King by name during his acceptance address.

"Black enough, white enough: the Obama dilemma,"—that's what Rickey Hendon has called this whole situation, as he and I held early morning political discussions after examining issues from the day before. Like when Bill Clinton made the statement after Barack won North Carolina's primary, that Jesse Jackson had carried the state in 1988. Rickey said, "Black enough, white enough, the Obama dilemma."

When Clinton referred to Barack as a "fairy tale," we concluded that white America couldn't believe that Barack was Black. We discussed often whether America was ready for a Black president.

I gave a Mother's Day speech this year at Christ Universal Temple in Chicago recognizing the historical moment, and a line in the speech was about the power and magic of a mother.

We are on the brink of America's first Black president, who has been delivered by a white woman. A white mother who made a choice, and sacrificed, to give her children the best education at the best schools. How powerful is that? Rickey's question was profound, "Black enough, white enough: the Obama dilemma."

In the primary debates, Barack shone as the bright, intelligent one, yet his candidacy was different. He had to walk the middle line, the tightrope, where he could not appear too Black or too white. He had to travel the center. Print stories appeared in the *New York Times*, "Is Obama the End of Black Politics?" and, "Where Whites Draw the Line." Are we looking at another standard? Was this racist, or just an honest discussion to be had?

The question was, how white or how Black. The question was, how much was enough, how much was too much, how much was not enough. This was clearly the Obama dilemma. I personally thought the dilemma was transforming, and thought that maybe America was ready to give up racism and allow a person of color to be recognized for service, intelligence, and deed, especially since Barack had resonated so well.

The Democratic primary was one race, and the race was on with Hillary Clinton as the major opponent. Racism and sexism were center stage. Neither candidate could be over-bearing and both had appeal. Hillary couldn't be the "little lady," and Barack couldn't be the "angry Black man."

But the general election was quite a different race, and the gloves have come off as both Obama/Biden and McCain/Palin engage the game to win. As much as Barack had tried to eliminate the race question in the past two years, Republicans will use the old fashioned scare tactics in new ways. But, what was different in the game of dirty tricks this time was that the Black candidate had enough money, status, and resources to play back.

For the first time ever, Oprah Winfrey, private citizen, endorsed Barack Obama. In doing so, she took a risk. Not everyone cheered. Her core audience, white women, felt that she had betrayed them by not supporting Hillary Clinton. Then later, Republican women were insisting that she have Sarah Palin as her guest before the general election. Oprah flatly refused. This was yet another case of "Black enough, white enough." But again, Oprah had ample resources within her organization to fight back and maintain her own.

As this book is being written, the political war is current. The polls show a statistical tie and this dead-heat election in November could go either Democratic or Republican. The economy is a disaster, two wars are on, Texas has flooded, and the candidates must address these hard issues as they try to rule the land. The campaign, with all of its political correctness and tiptoeing around explosive issues, has really now gotten down to—it's the economy stupid!—making and keeping the economy solid. The average John and Jane Doe are worried about keeping homes and jobs now more than anything else.

This race is impacted by the economy daily. In a historic Wall

Street dive that has America shaking in its boots, the economy has entered the campaign full blast as the investment banks have fallen. Lehman Brothers filed for bankruptcy and Merrill Lynch is being purchased by Bank of America. This is staggering news and we have yet to realize the true impact of the financial crisis—the worse since the Great Depression.

Clearly this disaster lies at the feet of the Republicans, which is good news for the Barack campaign. Perhaps this is a deciding factor, where race vanishes, as we look at the leadership of the country for viable economic solutions, making race a mute point.

Suddenly, Palin has disappeared from the front page and her foolishness and inexperience become transparent against real presidential issues, as the candidates now ponder the economic question.

This 2008 presidential race has been hot, inclusive, divisive, challenging, engaging, and will be studied for years to come. This book gives a first hand account to this history from day one with a direct perspective from Senator Rickey Hendon, who has witnessed the Barack rise. A new chapter in American politics has come about, as well as a new chapter in race relations. But the fundamental question throughout the race that started in Springfield, Illinois on February 10, 2007, has been and continues to be, Black enough, white enough? This is Barack Obama's dilemma, and he will answer it for years to come, by example. Win or lose.

*****

The Elephants Danced: A Political Parable
By Hermene D. Hartman

Once upon a time there was a group called the Frogs, a group of males who met regularly because some of the other animals in the concrete jungle wouldn't allow them in their organizations or at their events and functions. During this era of segregation, the Frogs were shut out. The Frogs set up their own meetings with other animals in the jungle to talk about the jungle business. Before long, the Frogs grew in their status and stature, so much so, that when the other animals wanted to do something important, they appeared before them.

As a matter of practice, the Frogs only attended to important jungle matters.

Two of the Frogs were in politics. They grew up to become Elephants. Both of the Elephants worked hard, toiling long in the forest to earn votes and the respect of family, friends, fellow politicians, and other jungle animals. Before long, they had seniority. They became powerful.

The two became rulers. When they moved, the jungle would shake and quake. One ruled the county part of the jungle. The other ruled the state part of the jungle. Although they were called presidents, they really were kings. The Elephant kings were of the same generation. They both had been groomed and trained by Irish Giraffes.

One Elephant king remained dependent on the Giraffes while the other Elephant king broke free. The dependent Elephant didn't really realize he was an Elephant king, but the Giraffes did. The Giraffes told him all the time that he was just part of a circus act, and he believed it.

He was an Elephant who acted like a frog. He jumped when the Giraffes said so. They gave him jobs, positions and contracts. He was grateful to the Giraffes. He groomed young frogs and baby Elephants. He put them in place.

Many thought the county Elephant king was tired, and some thought it was time for him to go lie down. But he didn't want the baby Elephants to suffer. He was afraid that if he moved out of place, the baby Elephants might lose their important and semi-powerful berths, he explained to the Frogs. So he stayed on to maintain the jungle.

The independent Elephant knew he was an Elephant. He knew he was a king. He shook the state earth sometimes to let them know he was there. He swung his trunk to see if the Giraffes would move to his beat. They did. He liked the Giraffes and knew they were necessary, but he didn't let the Giraffes boss him. He formed alliances and followed the rules and laws of the jungle just like all of the other animals. He had Lion friends. He had Frog friends. He made friends with all animals. But he realized his strength and power as an Elephant king. He protected the baby Elephants. He protected them and groomed them in the ways of the jungle. He had vision and foresight. He knew who he was and what he was.

One day a young Lion, a cub, wanted more territory in the jungle. He wanted to soar and roar. He was one of the smartest cubs the state jungle had seen. He was a model Lion. One day, he too would be a king. He was the next generation. He was the future. He could leave the state jungle and go to the national jungle. He might even go to the zoo in Washington and, one day, reign in the White House. He was that good.

The independent Elephant saw the possibilities and opportunities. He groomed him. He spoke to all of his animal friends about him. He encouraged the young Lion . He helped prepare him to rule. He told some of the other animals that were not behind the Lion, "if you don't support him you will feel my full Elephant weight."

The state Elephant king got it. He wanted to seize the day with his young cub. And he did. At election time the young cub won. He won big. All of the animals voted for him. Frogs, Cheetahs, Water Buffalos, Giraffes, Flamingoes, Lions, Tigers and Bears, oh my! All of the animals liked him. The cub ran on his merits and his brains. He wasn't afraid to walk in all parts of the jungle. He campaigned everywhere and he won. He is now hunting for larger prey. The Elephants danced in celebration of the Lion cub. Save one.

The county Elephant wanted to keep the jungle balanced with the Giraffes. He fretted about his baby Elephants. He insisted on supporting the baby Giraffe, who had challenged the young Lion.

The state Elephant saw it differently. He knew that one day the young Lion would be king of the jungle. "He belongs to us. He is our kin. He is our Lion," the state Elephant king said to the county Elephant king, then asked: "How long do you have to bow to the Giraffes? When do you stand up for your own? When do you use your Elephant power for yourself?"

The county Elephant held his head down as he appeared before the Frogs. He was stuck. He was old fashioned. He was from another time and another place. He still believed that the tallest animal in the jungle was king. He didn't think he could win without them. He was sometimes called Uncle Elephant or Boy Giraffe. The Giraffes had fed him at the trough for so many years.

The state Elephant stepped hard. The earth shook. He said it was time to move forward. "We can't always be looking up to the Giraffes. We have to be Elephants in our own right. We have to let the Lion run. The Lion must run fast and hard. He can be king of the jungle one day. As an Elephant, I must help him. It is my duty. I am not as tall as the Giraffe, but I am a mighty Elephant. Who won't get out of my way?"

The Elephants danced regarding the Lion. The Frogs watched and listened. One Frog said to the Elephants, "you have left us with two points of view. One independent. One dependent. One new. One old. We respect you both because you are two forces to be reckoned with. You both are too big for the Frogs to dance with. You both could hurt us."

But the other animals in the jungle voted for the young Lion. He won, he won big.

The Moral of the Story: Sometimes you can't dance with the one that brought you. Sometimes you've got to dance for yourself.

ONE

The Beginning of Barack Obama

My first recollection of meeting Barack Obama is a little fuzzy. I think it was during a voter registration drive in Chicago in the early 1990s called Project Vote. Project Vote was one of the first times people actually got paid to register new voters. There were both good things and bad things about this new program. I gladly took my dollar for every name I registered; that was big money for an outgoing, hard worker like me. That was the good part. The bad part came when the money ran out and nobody wanted to volunteer anymore.

Let me say up front that I did not start out as an Obama fan, nor am I a blindly loyal Barack supporter, now. I served with him in the Illinois Senate from 1996 until he moved to the United States Senate in 2004, and we occasionally had our differences. But the recent attacks on the senator along racial lines have made me a more fanatical Obamanite. The unwarranted attacks are the reason why I suggested this book to my friend, Hermene Hartman, the publisher of *N'DIGO* newspaper, an opinion leader for the African American community in Chicago and the first print media to cover Barack.

A close friend of mine, who is a fellow elected official, and I disagree about Barack on a regular basis. She doesn't want to hear anything unflattering about him—absolutely nothing. It's as if she has selective amnesia because we have all disagreed with Barack at times while debating issues in the State Senate. I believe an honest examination of those differences should be presented to the people of this country. I don't mean the senator any harm; in fact, I believe an open and honest discussion about Barack's votes in the Illinois Senate and positions he took will be good for Barack and good for America. How else will white Americans know that Barack Obama is no militant and Black Americans know that he is no sell out? At first, Black people

1

were questioning Barack's commitment, and then after he emerged, whites began looking at his blackness. Both groups wondered if he was a Muslim or Christian, and thus began what Hermene and I call "the Obama Dilemma."

Many Black people believe Barack Obama can do no wrong and some just want to see a Black President of the United States before they die, hence there will be some people who might find fault in what I have to say. If so, it won't be the first time one of our own has taken it on the chin for being seen as not worshipful enough. For example, take nationally acclaimed Black journalist and commentator Tavis Smiley. Tavis has taken considerable heat on Black radio for not supporting Obama. I know he isn't wild about Barack and said a few things on his show that offended some people. I didn't hear anything that offended me, but others were dismayed by his lack of solidarity. Barack has captured the hopes of many people, hopes that many African Americans thought they never dared to have in this lifetime, and now Tavis is being called a traitor and an Uncle Tom.

Imagine! Just recently, Tavis was a Black folk hero himself. His troubles with Black Entertainment Television (B.E.T.) network were the community's troubles. When the network fired him, many people supported him and vilified B.E.T. for dumping this icon of Black America. Many Black people loved Tavis—but now all of a sudden they don't.

And on the other side of the fence, some white people will take issue with this book because they believe America's racism is passé, and the brutality inflicted in the past is irrelevant to the America of today. But this is a frustrating delusion. The 1950s and 1960s are still an embarrassingly short time ago, and Black people are still being mistreated in this great country even as I write.

America's misguided perception of itself is evidenced by the words of Geraldine Ferraro. At one point in the Democratic primary campaign, she commented that Barack is lucky to be a Black man in America. How could anyone think it is lucky to be a Black man in America? I believe Ferraro knows better, but somebody had to do what Hillary Clinton, as a candidate, could not do, and that was to remind the American people that Senator Barack Obama is Black — even if he is only half Black. In the slave days, just one drop of Black blood made you Black as far as many legitimate governments and people were concerned, let alone those that dealt in slavery and racism, and the "one drop rule" is still very much in effect today.

Barack is caught between two worlds and struggles for acceptance by either side—Black enough? White enough? It's a fine line that he must walk. Barack's dilemma of being in the middle was evidence by Rev. Jesse Jackson's unfortunate "open mic" incident. Jesse was captured on tape saying that Barack was "talking down to Black people," implying that he was being condescending to Blacks in order to impress white voters. By not being Black enough or accepting of Black excuses, real or not, for what he considers unacceptable behavior, Barack gains white support, but risks losing Black supporters.

Reverend Jackson, my friend and one of America's greatest civil rights leaders, certainly made an audacious mistake in this incident, and even his own son, Congressman Jesse Jackson Jr., chastised him. Reverend Jackson's entire career will not and should not be judged by this one slip of the lip, but Barack needs to understand how Reverend Jackson feels about those days not long ago when Black people had to struggle for every little break, and his frustration with this modern perception that we are now responsible for our own troubles.

***

I have been an Illinois state senator since 1993, but I was never supposed to be a candidate for anything. I grew up on the West Side of Chicago, where my family moved after a brief stay in Alabama after my father died when I was only three years old. I was born on December 8, 1953 in Cleveland, Ohio. My parents, Jimmy and Olivia Hendon had moved there looking for work. My mother raised me and my three siblings, Ruby, Jimmy, and Barbara (now known as Shebeta) as a single parent. We never had much, and my mother was always the last one to eat, which taught me that your children come first. This instilled in me the desire to look out for other people and eventually led to my entry into politics.

I became increasingly involved in local politics as a young protégé of U.S. Congressman Danny Davis from the 7th District in Chicago and as a volunteer for Chicago's first Black mayor, Harold

Washington, during the 1980s. Harold's was a grassroots movement, and in those days, volunteers were enthusiastic and plentiful. Without volunteers, grassroots political movements die on the vine. I worked precincts and did fundraisers for independent Democrats including Harold and Congressman Davis, and Chicago aldermen Ed Smith and Wallace Davis, and many others. I became a Democratic committeeman in 1988 as the last political appointment Mayor Washington made before he died, and the succession debacle that followed his death convinced me to pursue higher office.

I ran successfully for alderman of the Chicago City Council in 1989, where I created the Affirmative Action Committee under the Budget Committee and began the clean up of the near West Side in which my ward was located. Under the Voting Rights Act, a new state Senate district was drawn for the West Side, and against all odds and facing an opponent with nearly $2 million to my $70,000, I became the senator for the new 5th district in 1993. I have been Assistant Majority Leader in the Illinois Senate since 2002 and was the youngest African American male to ever be named to the position. I am chairman of the most powerful committee, the Rules Committee, and I also chair the Executive Appointments Committee.

I credit all of my victories to the people who have supported me, especially in those early races, and I believe I have been successful in politics not because of pedigree or wealth, but because I call it like I see it. Some people like that about me, and others hate me for it, but 63 percent of the voters in my district, which is mostly African American, gave me their hope, faith and trust in my primary race this year.

But because of my habit of telling it like it is—as I see it—I'm not sure how many people are going to be happy with me for writing my controversial views on Senator Barack Obama, his run for the presidency, and the continuing issue of race in our country. My political godfather, Illinois Senate President Emil Jones Jr., is also Obama's political godfather. President Jones' muscle got Barack elected to the United States Senate in the first place, and I hope this great man—the only Black State Senate president in the entire country—will read this book with an open mind. Barack is a very special person to him, and I understand his desire to see him succeed.

This book has been compiled from a journal that I've kept of events and my opinions involving Barack's road to the White House, from the beginning of his run, when he announced his candidacy, to his acceptance speech after he secured the nomination at the Democratic National Convention in August 2008, to his ultimate historic victory. Since this book was written about events as they were unfolding, much of the discussion deals with issues and incidents that have long since been resolved, and perhaps even forgotten. But I think the memory of the hopes, the uncertainty, the tough choices, the curve balls and surprise game changers, and most of all, the nail biting stress of the past year should remain preserved just as it was, so this book will read as if the outcome is not yet known—as it was not at the time.

It gives my perspective as Barack's former and current colleague, especially as it relates to the fine line he has to walk in America because of his race. To whites and Blacks, race is never not a question in America, and throughout his candidacy, Barack took heat from both sides—when the real issues should have been about his character and ideas, and not the color of his skin.

TWO

Lightning in a Bottle

I was there on February 10, 2007 when U.S. Senator Barack Obama made his announcement to run for president in Springfield, Illinois, the state's capitol and the site where Abraham Lincoln expressed his own presidential aspirations. It was so cold that my toes were stuck together, but the Springfield plaza was absolutely packed with people and not a soul left until after the 20-minute speech. The chill from the cold was no match for the fire Barack lit in the hearts of everyone there. It was magic. I have been present for some powerful speeches in my life, but this one was different. Barack captured the winds of our times and delivered a speech that ignited the hopes of everyone there. The crowd was young and old, Black and white, and all solidly frozen—but not by the icy winter temperatures—by the mesmerizing power of a great speaker. I stood there in awe.

It was a life-changing moment for many of those who defied the bitter cold and hung onto Barack's every word that day. Nothing mattered but the tall, lanky young man from the Illinois Senate speaking from the same spot where President Lincoln once had. Senator Obama made people believe change was possible and that he would usher in a new age. Dick Durbin, Illinois' senior U.S. senator, did an excellent job of introducing the new presidential contender, and then Barack's speech took everyone's breath away.

I had been around Senator Obama for years by then, but this time he seemed larger than life, and I knew I was watching history in the making. Barack had captured lightning in a bottle. As I looked around the plaza packed with white people listening intently, I knew something phenomenal was happening, and it was an amazing feeling. I also felt the drama of the event through observing the high security and armed sharp shooters on every roof. The presence of such a large number of police and state troopers stunned me and reminded me that the America of the 1950s and the 1960s is not dead. The huge police presence reinforced the reality that Barack was putting his life on the line for all of us.

He gave a great speech, but I was very happy that he cut it short. As soon as he was done, we hurried to find coffee, hot chocolate, or anything that might warm up our chilled bones. My friend, State Senator Kimberly Lightford, waved to our former colleague, and we caught his eye as he and his wife, Michelle, were leaving the stage. As we made our way through the massive crowd, I noticed politicians who hated each other all united behind this new face. Democrats from completely different philosophies and opposing camps were standing together under a common cause. Political hacks and progressives were hand in hand. I knew then that Barack was going to become the next President of the United States.

Barack struck a chord with the American people like no other candidate since President John F. Kennedy. He and Michelle are now the Black Camelot, the new picture of hope, love, and power, and the American people needed something new. With two wars costing thousands of lives and billions of dollars, and neither with any end in sight; horrors such as thousands of people carelessly left stranded on the rooftops of a flooded city, and a collapsing economy, people want a Superman, a Luke Skywalker, a hero who can use the Force to defeat the darkness enveloping this great nation. Senator Barack Obama is in the right place at the right time with the right stuff—and I believed the presidency was his destiny.

Young people who had given up on this country suddenly became actively engaged in the political process. Poor people dared to have hope and are voted in records numbers. Money for Barack's campaign flowed in at record-breaking rates, but the key indicator was not the huge sums Barack raised, but the number of small donors who contributed. More people have given to Senator Obama than to any other candidate by far. He raised more money over the Internet than ever in history and headed towards breaking every record for raising money—without taking funds from Washington, D.C. lobbyists—unbelievable!

Ordinary working class people are giving up what little they have to a politician—that is lightning in a bottle and the stuff movements are made of. I saw this once before when Chicago elected its first Black mayor, our beloved Harold. Most of the money raised came in small increments at church rallies where Harold gave stirring speeches similar to those of Barack Obama. Harold went on to win—I fully expected Barack Obama to do the same.

***

I bought Barack's first book, *Dreams of My Father*, when he first arrived in the Illinois State Senate. I thought it would give me some insight into the man. He is a very complex and unique individual. Having an African father and a white mother from Kansas must have been a challenging identity. As I reflect back on his book, I can see that he knew a long time ago where he wanted to go in life. I heard the Clinton camp's claim that Barack wrote about becoming president as his goal in kindergarten, but so what? So did I. And I wrote about being a fireman, a police officer, and movie star, too. What's wrong with having dreams? I know Barack had big dreams and even bigger plans. He came to the State Senate highly opinionated, as did I, and just like me, he never accepted the freshman label or played the freshman role. Make no mistake, this man is a politician, bright and genuine though he may be.

I believe that the beginning of a political career is a significant period in a politician's life that can tell us much about him or her. Interestingly, Barack Obama's political career began with a misunderstanding—although some have called it by much nastier names, but I won't venture into that tall grass. Back in 1996, while Barack was in Chicago practicing law, an Illinois state senator named Alice Palmer made plans to run for United States Congress in the 2nd District, replacing the disgraced incumbent, Mel Reynolds, who resigned his office and went to prison because of a sex scandal involving an underage campaign volunteer. Alice thought she was going to win Reynolds' seat and supposedly had a tacit agreement to have Barack Obama run for what was to be her vacated State Senate seat once she went to congress. Jesse Jackson Jr., Illinois State Senator Emil Jones and

State Representative Monique Davis were also in that congressional race, which Jesse Jr. won to become Congressman Jesse Jackson Jr.

When Alice lost, she then wanted to return to her State Senate seat. The filing period for the election for her seat immediately followed the congressional race, and she had to scramble to get on the ballot to run for re-election. There are two sides to every story, and in politics there are sometimes even more than that, but all I know is that Alice and Barack both filed to run for the office on the same day and both had collected signatures to get on the ballot. One of Barack's campaign advisors, Alan Dobry, who had been Alice's campaign manager in previous elections, challenged Alice's signing petitions. Her petitions were found to be inadequate, and she was knocked off the ballot. The sitting senator, the incumbent, was kicked off the ballot. I don't believe that had ever happened before in Illinois.

Now, there is nothing wrong with knocking someone off the ballot. As it happened, I was at the Chicago Board of Elections examining petitions that my own opponents had filed because I was going to try to kick them off the ballot, just as they were trying to kick me off the ballot, when I ran into some of Alice's supporters. They were going through someone's petition, which was not at all unusual. I was on friendly terms with them, but when I passed their table, their behavior seemed suspicious. They were deliberately covering up the name of the candidate whose petition they were examining.

Being Rickey Hendon, I just lifted up the paper to see who it was. When I saw Alice's name, I thought I was going to die! I called Alice and told her that her own supporters were going through her petitions, and she didn't believe me. Now, Barack has continually denied having had anything to do with knocking Alice off the ballot. And I can say that I saw, with my own eyes, Alice's own supporters examining her petitions.

Dobry also kicked two perennial candidates off the ballot by challenging their signatures, and Barack ran unopposed in the primary, and later in the general election, and attained his first elected office. But, no one thinks Barack could have ever beaten Alice Palmer.

A lot of Black activists and politicians were upset over this episode of intrigue; everybody loved Senator Palmer and her husband, Buzz. They were progressive, intellectual thinkers and both were highly

10

respected throughout the independent political community. Many Black leaders on the South Side of Chicago felt resentment towards this new upstart, Barack Obama. Senator Palmer was not happy about the way things turned out back then, and I'm sure I saw her posing for pictures at a campaign event for Senator Hillary Clinton during the Democratic Primary race a few months ago.

I clearly can't criticize Barack for having ideas and being aggressive, but there were times when he supported challenges to Senate President Emil Jones' authority and strategies. In the summer of 2004, we were in the middle of a serious dispute between our governor, Rod Blagojevich, and Speaker of the House Michael Madigan. Compounding the conflict was the fact that Speaker Madigan was also the Chairman of the Illinois State Party. Things got so bad none of our leaders were speaking to each other at the 2004 Democratic National Convention. In fact, we went into overtime that year and only got out of session so that senators could attend the convention. I myself was so sick of politicians by that time I didn't even go. I heard that the governor, the speaker and the Senate president all had parties at the convention and none attended the others' party.

Illinois Democrats must have appeared to be totally dysfunctional to our national party leaders. For the first time in 26 years, we controlled the Governor's office, the Illinois House and the Illinois Senate, we even controlled most of Constitutional Offices, yet we couldn't pass a budget or move forward an agenda. We all became restless and frustrated. At one point, some white senators demanded that Senate President Jones dump his support for the governor, and support Speaker Madigan, which would have, in effect, given the speaker control over both chambers.

One day in caucus, things got really heated and a mini-rebellion was launched. It was led by one of Barack's white poker buddies, and Barack echoed his sentiments. Several members of the Black Caucus, a group of Black senators of which Barack was a member, asked that Barack check himself. I then challenged the other rebels to speak up and choose sides. The room went silent, and the overthrow fizzled out. But I never forgot seeing how Barack had had the courage to speak when others clung to the shadows.

But, from the very beginning, Barack demonstrated ambition.

In 2000, less than four years after being elected to the State Senate, Barack made another move and ran for a seat in Congress against incumbent Congressman Bobby Rush. My best friend, State Senator Donne Trotter, who was already in the contest against Rush, thought Barack believed he could force him out of the race. Donne had been in the Illinois House and Senate for over a decade and he clearly resented this new guy attempting to jump over him.

With two state senators in the race there was no way that either one was going to beat Congressman Rush. I tried to talk to both of them, but neither one would drop out. I eventually lent my name to Donne's campaign, endorsing him, even though I still had a good relationship with Rush. I had supported him when he ran for mayor against Chicago's Richard M. Daley, even though all of Rush's close political allies abandoned him.

In his 2000 re-election bid, Congressman Rush avoided all debates and forums—he used the old "Rose Garden Strategy" and it worked. At every event, senators Obama and Trotter were left to attack each other and Rush cruised to victory by about a two-to-one margin.

But Barack clearly had higher aspirations and had no time to wait. In 2004, he reached for the United States Senate, and this time good fortune smiled on him. In the primary, Barack was running third behind front-runner Blair Hull and Dan Hynes, when Hull's sealed divorce papers became public. A controversy ensued, and Barack surged to the front and won the nomination.

In the general election, Barack faced Republican Jack Ryan, who was the front-runner until details of his messy divorce, involving sex clubs, landed in the media. Ryan dropped out of the race. When Illinois Republican Party then brought in a carpetbagger from Maryland, Black Republican Alan Keyes, to replace Ryan against Barack Obama— pitting two African Americans against each other, as if any old Black man could substitute for another—Keyes was so out-of-the-box that Obama won the Illinois seat in a landslide, even garnering a significant number of Republican votes.

Barack's career started with a break—an overconfident candidate planned a little too far ahead, and Barack was the beneficiary—and since then, it seems that luck had always been with him. Every time he has made a move for a higher office, his current position has been safe because he has always been in the middle of his term. But this just proves that he can be a careful, calculating Head of State. In politics, timing is everything, and Barack's timing has been impeccable. He has led a charmed political life.

THREE

Iowa: America's Wakeup Call

I was so proud of white people after Senator Obama won the Iowa caucus to start the year on January 3, 2008. My view of America was changed forever. I know exactly what Michelle Obama was trying to say when she said, "...for the first time in my adult lifetime, I am really proud of my country..." Barack's enemies tried to twist the comment to make her appear unpatriotic, but he stood behind his wife and supported her while she withstood attack after attack because of her statement. But most people knew exactly what she meant. Michelle clearly loves America and she was being honest.

There have been plenty of times when I have been disappointed in the leadership of our nation and the direction in which we were headed. I didn't say "for the first time," but I did tell an audience how proud I was of my country that night. I had never seen acceptance of one of us by white people at the level Barack experienced with the Iowa caucuses.

I do believe some people in the Obama camp got carried away after the victory, but I kept relatively calm—something that seems too good to be true could be a fluke. But even if Barack had never won another primary, I was impressed enough to savor the memory forever. Despite Iowa's history of independence and progressive thinking, many people believed he would lose this state. I thought he would do well— but I didn't know it would be that good! America climbed a major hurdle in race relations and showed the world our true colors that day, and began to answer one of the questions imbedded in our title—is Barack Obama white enough?

I was watching TV as the votes came in and almost cried. Not for Barack, but for the Dr. Kings, Shirley Chisholms, and ordinary, everyday Black people who thought they would never see a day like this. I'm from the West Side of Chicago, which is a very tough area, and it takes a lot to make me cry, but Black people's pride at the complete acceptance of Barack Obama as Iowa's choice was exhilarating—some were dancing in the streets. We all understood Michelle's words perfectly.

The people of Iowa put consideration of race in its proper place. Race or gender should never disqualify a person from serving. Race has always been the reason or excuse used by racists to leave African Americans in positions of permanent inferiority. The people of Iowa gave me hope.

One reason I believe Barack won Iowa is because of the caucuses in which people sit around and discuss the candidates and their views. In this forum, white voters get to know Senator Obama for the moderate that he is—and he is a moderate. Barack Obama is no Al Sharpton or Jesse Jackson, in my opinion. He is not radical, or even close to being a Black activist of any kind. Obama is absolutely no threat to white America or the status quo. I believe the voters in Iowa got it right—Obama is the right candidate for President of the United States.

I had to ask myself, what makes the people of Iowa so different, so much more progressive than the rest of America? I'm also wondering why Barack does much better in the smaller, traditionally red states than Senator Hillary Clinton. It seems the more people get to see Obama for themselves, the better he does. Many Americans get all of their political "insights" from the news or from the spin doctors, and we get presidents like George W. Bush as a result.

Iowa served as a wake up call to Americans on all fronts. It woke up Democrats, Republicans, and dreamers. Here was a Black presidential candidate to be taken seriously! Though many racial attacks have been aimed at Barack since January, Iowa still stands as a shining example of how far we have come.

FOUR

New Hampshire: Tears on Her Pillow

Barack lost the New Hampshire primary to Hillary Clinton on January 8, 2008. First, let me admit that I have always loved the former First Lady. I met her at the beginning of Bill Clinton's presidency when she was pushing hard to get universal health care for all Americans. I believed this to be a noble thing for her to attempt to accomplish. All people need and deserve health care; it is appalling that everyone doesn't have access to affordable health care here in the richest country in the world. I met Hillary at Miles Square Health Clinic on Chicago's West Side and found her to be both warm and sincere, and a breath of fresh air. All of the health care activists I knew expressed the same wonderful feelings about her.

As soon as I saw the tears welling up in Hillary's big sad eyes after she lost the Iowa caucus, I knew Barack was in trouble in New Hampshire, the next primary, which was being held the next week. In addition to Hillary's well-documented tears the night before the election, there was New Hampshire's history of going in a different direction than Iowa. Also, the "fate accompli" attitude of the Obama campaign did not help at all. Some of his handlers were so giddy that it came across as arrogance. Barack should have continued to act like the underdog. The front-runner always comes under attack from everyone who is serious about victory. Why wear that flak jacket before you have to? The Democratic presidential nomination contest was most certainly not over after only one primary, not with all these well paid media consultants and drama coaches around.

I watched the clips as Hillary choked up before that group of mostly women and said, "I just don't want to see us fall backwards,"

17

when she was talking about the "false hopes" offered by Obama. Despite her tears, Hillary found enough composure to turn around and knock Barack in the next breath by saying, "Some of us are right and some of us are wrong. Some of us are ready, and some of us are not."

Crocodile tears? Now, I don't know if the tears were planned or just prepared for, but it was brilliant theater, worthy of praise. If it was concocted, it was played to perfection and she deserves an Oscar. I honestly almost cried with her and I surely felt her pain. This was personal, and it hit home. I knew if I wept, others across America must have gotten a catch in the throat. It was a Kodak moment. Those warm, motherly tears visibly moved her questioner, and it was a perfect picture.

Senator Clinton made an emotional connection with the voters that day. Before this incident, her enemies had successfully, though wrongly, painted her as uncaring, cold and arrogant. When she wept, we saw a serious swing in the white female vote in her direction. Many of those votes had likely been with Barack Obama.

I sincerely hope it was genuine. I'm in politics, so I don't take much on face value. I knew one candidate who faked a stroke right before all of his elections to get the sympathy vote. It happened so regularly that we began to warn voters to expect it. He was miraculously cured once we exposed his sad ploy.

In politics, you sometimes just don't know what is real or not. Remember how in the film *Wag The Dog* the spin doctors created a phony war to rally support from the American people for an unpopular president? It easily could have been a true story—some media consultants actually steer campaigns through lies and deceit, and some people, in a quest for power will stop at nothing. I'm not accusing Hillary's camp of anything, but her tears struck me as great theater and made great TV.

Politics is draped in theater. One reason Obama has led most of the way through this campaign is his ability to deliver a great speech. Don't be naive enough to believe he wrote every word. His job is to deliver those words with heartfelt sincerity and nobody does it better. Hillary does not write all of her own speeches or position papers either. Much of what we say is written and rehearsed like a Broadway production, especially at that level.

If the entire episode was staged, someone certainly earned his or her money. Women rallied to her cause in New Hampshire and she won that primary. Even though Obama was leading in all the polls and Hillary seemed doomed, she won New Hampshire and the title once held by her husband, Bill, "The Comeback Kid." Now, she may have sincerely broken down, because as a female candidate, I know her advisors must have warned her about appearing weak. We are at war and America remains a male dominated country. We will never know, but personally, as a political junkie, I actually enjoyed the moment.

I still like Hillary a great deal. Unlike most of my colleagues, I am willing to look past some of the political rhetoric and focus on the woman I know. I also admire her husband, Bill. You can't be the "Comeback Kid" without having gone down at some point and bounced back, so the "Comeback Kid" is always a hero.

The Obama campaign is well aware of the determination of the Clintons. They seem ready to fight all the way to the convention if necessary.

FIVE

Is He Black Enough?
An African American Agenda

Barack Obama has Black blood running through his veins. For some people, that is enough to disqualify him from being our next president. Race should not be a factor one way or another, but in this case it is—to Obama's detriment. We know Barack is too Black for some white people, and that his race is the sole reason why they will reject him in favor of anybody, including the devil himself. But what about Black leaders who simply aren't with Obama? His agenda on issues important to Black people should be the determining factor as to his being Black enough, not raw politics.

I just saw the Black mayor of Philadelphia, Michael Nutter, who is supporting Hillary Clinton in the Pennsylvania primary that is only three weeks away on April 22. Several commentators have stated that Nutter's support of Clinton is interesting because Black voters put him in the mayor's office, and they are supporting Obama. One pundit suggested that Mayor Nutter would be in serious trouble when he comes up for re-election. When I listened to the mayor, it was obvious that he doesn't care what may happen to him in the future. Perhaps Obama supported a different candidate in Nutter's race for mayor, and this is his payback. In the game of politics, payback is always a possibility. Obama is not above the normal game of politics; he plays the game and he plays it well, and has supported white candidates over Black candidates, too.

On April 4, I returned to the Illinois State Capitol, where Obama got his start. I couldn't help but wonder if he missed this place. We are

21

fighting with the Republicans in the State Senate, and also have infighting continuing here in Illinois among us Democrats. Naturally, our Republican colleagues are attempting to fuel the fire so they can reap the benefits. This is the same thing that is happening on the national scene. Hillary continues to attack Barack, and he is forced to fire back, while John McCain sits on the sidelines and watches with glee. This Democratic self-destruction must be making him feel confident. The longer it lasts, the worst it gets for the two Democrats, and then nobody on the Democratic side wins.

A new person attacking Barack now is a Black congressman from Missouri, Emanuel Cleaver. I saw Congressman Cleaver on television mocking Barack's style of speech. He claimed that Barack doesn't speak like Black people. He basically said that Barack is too polished, or too white. His position on this non-issue of speaking style was aimed at the Barack's blackness. He was indirectly saying that Barack is not Black enough. Of course, Cleaver is a supporter of Hillary Clinton, and, to me, the funny thing is that Congressman Cleaver's style of speech and clean-cut look are very similar to Obama's. He sounded quite proper and upper crust to me, so how can he say Barack is not fire and brimstone when he himself chooses a more subtle style? I am fire and brimstone, so I know it when I see it and just concede different strokes for different folks.

You would think the Clinton campaign would have used someone with the "Black" style they claim Barack lacks to launch this attack, but maybe their cupboard is getting thin. I guess they had to "leave it to Cleaver"—a well-polished, highly-educated Black man—to attack Barack on being too well polished. I can't assume that Cleaver doesn't have a legitimate reason to oppose Barack, but he failed to state one, and a few days later, he was on TV backpedaling from his comments. I guess he heard from some of his constituents from the great state of Missouri.

Congressman Stephanie Tubbs Jones from Ohio also posed the question of whether Barack Obama is Black enough. (Tubbs Jones passed away after I made these notes and before this book was published.) She was on stage with Hillary Clinton the night of the Ohio primary on March 4. Senator Clinton won Ohio with the help of Representative Tubbs Jones. It will be interesting to see how these distinguished Black officer holders fair in their next elections, especially if Barack Obama becomes President of the United States. At the very least, I guarantee they will draw a Black opponent in their next elections, and that opponent will use this issue against them with Black and independent voters. Someone is going to have a lot of explaining to do. Their core constituents are going to be angry with them.

Barack can get his dander up at times as well, but knowing him, he will forgive and forget, and attempt to work with all of the Black elected officials who supported candidates other than him. Either way, it will be interesting to follow up on the outcome and see if there is a price to pay at the polls down the road.

***

The commemoration of the assassination of the great Dr. Martin Luther King Jr. took place on April 4. Who told Barack to be anywhere other than Memphis? John McCain was there in Memphis, apologizing for his opposition to making Dr. King's birthday a holiday. Hillary Clinton was there in Memphis, in a Black church, an institution she knows well. Where in the hell was Barack Obama? Very few people would argue that Dr. Martin Luther King Jr. was the greatest civil rights leader of all time. Why didn't someone convince Barack to go to Memphis? It would have said to the people who wonder if he's Black enough, that he is—or at least that he will try to be.

Several television commentators mentioned his absence on various talk shows. They showed him making a speech somewhere and mentioning Dr. King's life and untimely death, but they brought up the fact that he did not go to the Lorraine Hotel or stand on the balcony. Now, wouldn't that have been the photo of a lifetime? What a better opportunity to say to Black people that he really cares about their plight, with the cover of a respected national hero to protect him from any white backlash.

These are the kind of missteps that give Black Clinton supporters room to operate. They can bring up things like Memphis and the Jena 6 in their arguments and have a leg to stand on. The Obama campaign cannot take the Black vote for granted. If Barack won't espouse an urban agenda, he should at least show some respect for our struggles, both present and past.

At some point, the question of Obama's blackness must be measured against an African American agenda. All candidates should have to address the needs and concerns of the Black community if they are seeking our votes. The problems within the Black community are too great to be ignored and too urgent to be put on hold. Real "change" in America cannot be addressed without dealing with this truth. Black people should be more concerned with what Obama thinks than how he looks.

From the time I began voting, I have tried to learn about candidates and how they personally think about issues that are important to me: my family, and our future. The Black agenda includes, but is not limited to: fairness, equal rights, economic development and ending police brutality. Reparations for slavery is still high on the Black agenda, and I believe Congressman John Conyers of Michigan and other brave legislators deserve credit for keeping this issue alive. After all, it seems that everybody gets reparations except Black people here in the country we certainly helped build without any compensation. The fact is, forced Black labor for over 400 years made America a rich nation.

I know Barack will never speak out on many of these issues before November, but perhaps his conscience will lead him to address them after he becomes the president. Senator Clinton and even Senator John McCain should also be presented with questions relating to our plight in America, not just Senator Obama.

How Black does the man have to be to satisfy the more radical members of the Black community? One can argue that if Barack brought forth an urban agenda, his candidacy would be doomed. I don't like it, but I do understand his growing dilemma—he is damned if he does and damned if he doesn't.

Obama is in a real quagmire, which is quickly approaching a boiling point. So far, he has balanced both sides of this continual racial divide with skills beyond his limited political experience. If he talks about his upbringing, someone will find fault—as if any of us has say in whom our parents are.

The first thing I heard on Black FM radio on the morning of April 7 was about Barack not going to Memphis to commemorate the assassination of Dr. King. This was my first time hearing the issue on

Black hip hop radio. The responses called in by the listeners were quite interesting—three out of four, or 75 percent, said he did not have to go, and back off! Well, usually, 75 percent sounds good, but not in this case. To have 25 percent of your base wondering about your commitment to them could doom your candidacy.

I feel that Barack should have been the first person in Memphis, and while I'm okay with it, I'm not so sure about my people, though. One reason I'm writing this book is to help people understand Barack, and I truly believe that Barack knows who he is and he cares about Black people, his strongest base. Everybody has a base or core group of die-hard supporters, and this is not at the exclusion of anyone else who may be supportive of the same candidate. When building on his larger coalition of voters, Barack needs to be careful to not offend his base.

If one out of every four African American voters—or 25 percent—rejects Obama, he cannot win. So far, he has received an average of around 85 percent of the Black vote; he got 90 percent in Mississippi and was in the 90 percent range in Chicago and Black neighborhoods in every state. I'm not suggesting my friend needs or will even heed my advice, but he needs to retain at least 80 percent of the Black vote.

The other thing I noticed on the radio was the number of young people calling in. This is certainly Barack's base, and all races of young people listen to Black radio. As a student of politics and an Obama supporter, I hope he doesn't forget to solidify his base and not alienate his main, most reverent supporters. This mistake has been made before in many other campaigns. I pounded my base in my last election with great results—around 88 percent of the Black vote.

***

On April 19, I received an email from a dear friend on the West Coast containing an article written by Betty Pleasant of the *Los Angeles Sentinel*. It was about the Black newspaper publishers' dissatisfaction with the Obama campaign. The article is dated April 15, 2008, and to sum it up, 15 Black newspapers are claiming to have been snubbed by the Obama campaign—no interviews and no advertising dollars, period. The National Newspaper Publishers Association—the Black publishers' trade group—met with all three campaigns on March 13, the article says, and they talked about participation and access. They got the same treatment from all of them, including their brother Barack, according to the Black publishers. They claim to have been lied to and ignored by the candidates.

The Black press is the backbone, the anchor, the one of the most important institutions in the Black community, in my opinion. Everybody does not go to the Black church, the other source of important information for Black people, but we all read papers or listen to Black radio, be it hip hop or gospel.

The email quotes several Black newspaper publishers who expected disdain from the Republicans and other Democrats, but not the Black Democrat. And it does not help that all reports say Barack is flush with cash. You can't just talk about economic development and not put your money where your mouth is.

I guess the publishers felt the way I did the day a large group of Illinois Black elected officials endorsed Barack at a press conference in his office. Obama was campaigning elsewhere, but the love fest went on for our native son and brother. When the press conference was over I asked for a few buttons. I, the Assistant Majority Leader of the Illinois State Senate, was given one button.

When I picked up two more, I was stared at as if I was the local wine head who just crashed the party! A lovely lady eased over and explained to me that I would have to pay for the other two buttons I had just picked up. She asked for two dollars apiece! I've paid for buttons before, but not from a serious campaign. I've bought them from vendors trying to make a living that I was trying to help out, or folks who made unique buttons that I liked. Okay, what the heck is a couple of bucks? But what bothered me most was the fact that my office had been pleading for material for weeks and we were hustling our butts off for Barack!

I ended up buying maybe a couple of hundred buttons for my volunteers and left shaking my head. We all knew Barack was going to win in his home state. We knew we were being written off and understood why, but it still didn't feel right. I guess his handlers thought, "Why buy the milk when you can get it free." Why spend any money in Illinois where you got it made? I knew his operation didn't spend much on any Black media here, but I didn't know there was a national pattern until now. Barack should buy every type of Black media in every upcoming primary.

All of the remaining contests are going to be squeakers, and ignoring his base could be hazardous to his campaign. Perhaps they think our papers can continue giving him headlines without paper and ink. I don't know, but I still punched holes in my favorite suit in order to wear my Barack button.

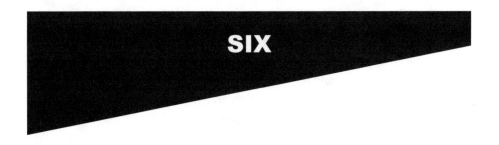

Is He White Enough?
A Personal Confrontation

One day after a tough vote on the Senate floor, Barack threatened to whip my ass—his words. I have previously refused to talk about this incident, but I'm writing about it now because I consider it proof positive that Barack is white enough to be President of the United States of America.

Times were tough. The State of Illinois was in financial trouble, and the then governor, George Ryan, had to cut numerous programs in order to balance the budget. Everyone knew the governor didn't want to close much needed facilities, but our fiscal outlook was very bleak and the War on Terrorism was draining resources and stalling any rebound.

The Republicans were in the majority, so their districts were spared; the brunt of the cuts were in Democratic districts or areas where they affected poor people the most. When the list of the cuts came out, I was outraged. They were cutting public health, child welfare programs, mental health, afterschool programs, drug abuse counseling, and other extremely important programs.

I had been through two nationally publicized tragedies in my district involving children left home alone in filth and squalor. The first case, in 1994, was the Keystone 19. The Illinois Department of Children and Family Services took 19 young children and babies away from their absent or drug addicted parents in a small house on Keystone Street.

I went to the house and almost gave up my lunch because of the garbage and human excrement all over the place. I had never seen such horrible living conditions in my entire life. I pic ked up one baby crawling in the filth and handed her to my administrative assistant, who was already feeding another hungry baby. It was so nasty, my other assistant got into an altercation with the only adult present that we found in a drunken stupor in a back bedroom.

The stench of old urine forced us to open every window. The police arrived and demanded that we leave because criminal charges were being filed and this was a crime scene. I identified myself, which made them no difference at all. They already knew who I was and they were angry at me for pointing out to the media that thugs were selling drugs right in front of the house 24/7.

I had some of the children's responsible relatives with me and we agreed to leave, but not without the remaining children who weren't home when the state raided the house. The police finally agreed to let us take the babies after the news reporters on the scene began filming the confrontation. After a lot of negative press for demanding that the children be placed with relatives, and numerous family court appearances on behalf of those hard-working, loving relatives, we were able to get most of the children placed with them. Many Chicagoans acted as if the entire family was on drugs, and that none of them should get their nieces and nephews, but I refused to just have them institutionalized with strangers when there were non-addicted family members who sincerely wanted the children.

Sometime later in my district, we had another incident of children left home alone in filth. This one was called the Huron 12, and the scenario was exactly the same—drug dealers operating with impunity on every corner, addicted parents, vomit, mice, and me. My heart was broken and I cried for these poor defenseless children. This case was sadder because there weren't as many loving relatives willing and able to step in.

I was depressed for months about these two episodes, knowing that they represented many, many others similar situations that avoided the headlines, but were just as tragic. My district on the West Side of Chicago has more of these types of cases than anywhere else in the entire state, so I was stunned when I saw that they were closing the only child welfare office on the West Side during this particular session of Governor Ryan's budget cuts. When I pleaded with the governor, all he could say to me was, "I'm sorry." Well, that wasn't good enough for me, and I began a crusade to keep the child welfare office with the greatest caseload open.

On the day the proposed cuts came to the Senate floor I had come to terms with the fact that my children were going to lose because the Republican senators were going to side with their Republican governor. I voted against the draconian cuts, and when the most vital child welfare office was about to be voted closed, I gave the most passionate speech of my life.

Speakers on the Republican side of the aisles sympathized with me, but as expected, they all voted "yes" to close the office. What I did not expect was that four Democrats voted "yes" along with the Republicans, including the only Black senator to vote against me, Barack Obama.

I was flabbergasted. I sat there stunned for a minute and then I went to the row of Democrats who voted with the Republicans and asked them why did they do it? All four sat next to each other in what we called Liberals Row, and they were considered to be fair-minded progressives, which added to my confusion and consternation.

The first senator I asked gave me an honest answer; it was political, but I accepted it because it was honest. The next senator said he wasn't paying attention and just voted with the row. A former senator, who I had helped a great deal with her domestic partnership legislation, simply apologized and asked for my forgiveness.

I went right down Liberal Row and finally arrived at my friend Barack's desk. He was running for the United States Senate at the time, and when I asked him with my sad eyes and perplexed, torn heart, he told me he did it because, "We have to be fiscally prudent," he said.

I said, "Huh?" And he explained to me that we had to show fiscal responsibility during tough budget times. Before I could ask him about the poor children, I found myself walking back to my seat in a daze. I sat down in a daydream, or nightmare, kind of blur and continued to vote "no" on cut after cut along with all the Democrats, including Liberal Row.

Finally, I heard the bill number for a cut on the South Side in Senator Obama's district. Barack rose to his feet, and towering over the Senate, gave a heart wrenching speech condemning this particular cut.

He asked for compassion and understanding. Now, this facility they wanted to close was very similar to the one he just voted to close on the West Side. His fiscally prudent vote took place only about 10 minutes earlier and now he wants compassion!

But the Republicans gave him the same rehearsed B.S. answer they gave me, and then I was recognized to speak on the closure. I said, "I am going to vote with my friend from the South Side because he is right—the need is great and the children are suffering. But it would have been nice if the senator had felt that same compassion for the children on the West Side that he so eloquently displays right now when it comes to the children in his district."

The vote was taken and Barack lost just like all of us Democrats lost that day. I voted with Barack as he watched to the roll call in amazement. Then, I sat there and watched as he pondered his next move. Finally, he got the attention of the presiding officer and asked that his vote be changed on the West Side closure from "yes" to "no."

He got into a brief procedural argument over the issue, but was told that he was too late to change his vote, and besides he had offered no explanation for his demand, such as a malfunction or accidentally pushing the wrong button.

Barack was totally pissed off now and he walked menacingly towards my seat on Leaders Row. His long, lanky body towered over me as I sat quietly seething within myself, worried about the children I knew were still living in despair back home in Chicago. I was mad at the Republicans, not Barack, but I sure as hell wasn't about to take any of his mess, not that day!

Barack leaned over and stuck his jagged, strained face into my space and told me in an eerie, dark voice that came from some secret place within the ugly side of him, "You embarrassed me on the Senate floor and if you ever do it again I will kick your ass!"
I said, "What?"

He said, "You heard me, [expletive], and if you come back here by the telephones, where the press can't see it, I will kick your ass right now!"

I stacked my few papers quietly on my desk in front of me and said, "Okay, [expletive], let's go."

I walked the few feet to the telephone area with his long legs swiftly pounding behind me. When we got there, I turned and put up my dukes like Muhammad Ali. I begged him to hit me and told him I couldn't go back to the West Side if I let a South Sider punk me and kick my butt. I swelled my five-foot-seven frame to about six feet and got up in his chest. A little pushing and shoving occurred, laced with profanity too vulgar to write, from both of us, until Senator Donne Trotter and others separated us.

Barack then invited me to come outside where he said he would stomp me into oblivion. I nodded my head and said, "Let's go." But before we could get out of the small room, Senate President Emil Jones demanded that I act like a leader and go back to my seat.

I gave Barack a few more choice words and told him I would see him later, but I did go back and sat down. Jones then warned Barack about starting fights he didn't need while running for higher office. Barack huffed and puffed and sneered at me as he passed my desk, but he, too went to his seat.

Andy Shaw, from Chicago TV's ABC-7, and a newspaper reporter noticed the commotion. They interviewed Barack, who soft-pedaled the entire incident and said we had kissed and made up. I refused to talk about it, but I made it clear that I had nothing to apologize for, and we had not made amends, regardless of what Barack said. They went back to Barack with my denial, and he was not happy. He walked over to my seat again and leaned over to say something to me.

I yelled to President Jones three seats down from me that he better come get his guy out my face. President Jones jumped up and took Barack off the floor, probably into his office so he could regain his much heralded composure.

Barack and I never talked about it again, but in this incident, he proved himself to be bi-partisan enough and white enough to be President of the United States of America to me.

Consider that Barack challenged a Black politician to a fistfight—a Black politician that some people consider to be a radical. In doing that, he was willing to put his life on the line for his beliefs. He voted along with the fiscal conservatives in Illinois. He went along with a Republican governor, and was the only Black state senator to do so, when it came to voting for closing a facility in the Black community.

How's that for proof in just one incident that Barack is independent enough in his thinking to be attractive to whites?

I also mention our confrontation as proof that Barack will be more than willing to use physical force to defend America if necessary. In addition to the discussion on whether he's Black enough or white enough, there has also been a lot of talk out there about whether Barack is tough enough to be president. Will he fight? If we were attacked by terrorists, would he pull the trigger? There's no doubt that he would.

With McCain being a war hero, people will try to use the toughness issue against Barack. So, I'm telling the story to show that yes, Barack will not hesitate to fight on behalf of the United States if it comes down to it, just as he tried to fight me because of his personal beliefs.

In other instances, Barack supported a white man for mayor over a Black female candidate, and he supported a Latino for City Clerk over another Black woman seeking that office. Is that white enough? I judge a politician by his or her actions, and who a politician supports, and why, should be very important to the public, it can tell you a lot about that person.

In this case, it proves that Barack never considers race in his decision making process. Some people criticized Obama for not supporting enough Black candidates in big races. I supported both of the Black women he rejected and I did not accept his reasons for doing so. I haven't always supported the Black candidate either, but I've always had a pretty good reason when I didn't.

But, it may not matter how much Barack shows his white side to some white people. The governor of Pennsylvania, Ed Rendell, has said that white men will not vote for Obama. And when Rendell said it, he did not flinch or attempt to sugarcoat his opinion. It is clear that even being half white is not white enough for some people.

Barack's mother was white and his father Black. He has the experiences of both worlds inside him. He does not run or hide from either side of his heritage. I, for one, am very proud of him for that. He knows who he is and he recognizes that he belongs to both worlds. But, more importantly, when will we get to the point where it does not matter?

Governor Rendell will deliver Pennsylvania to Hillary Clinton in a few weeks, but it won't be enough to put her over the top. I hope his statement about white men not voting for Barack only pertains to the primary election; if not, we are in big trouble. I guess we may as well go back to segregation if his statements are still true in 2008.

There is good news out of Pennsylvania, however. Bob Casey, Pennsylvania's U. S. Senator, is supporting his colleague Senator Obama. Senator Casey is well respected around the country, and his support should keep things close. The Clinton camp needs a large victory, and the polls show Barack closing fast; in fact, one poll has him within single digits. A small win by Hillary would be a big boost for Obama, who was trailing by as many as 18 points a few weeks ago, but I believe Obama will win a considerable percentage of the white vote in the rest of the states with upcoming primaries.

When Barack did not go to the biggest Black historical occasion of the year, the commemoration of the assassination of the greatest Black man of our times, Dr. King, perhaps he actually needed to be on the campaign trail, however, some have speculated about it being part of a strategy to let white voters know that "Black" is not a priority with him. If it isn't, he certainly passes the test of being white enough.

The dilemma Barack finds himself in has never been managed as well as he is handling it. He can bring people together without prejudice of any kind and he thinks for himself, which should help get him pass the race litmus test.

SEVEN

VWB (Voting While Black): Obama's State Senate Voting Record

For the most part, as an Illinois state senator, Barack Obama voted the Democratic Party line, as did I. He did show an occasional independent streak, but never for more than a vote or two. President Emil Jones runs a pretty tight ship. Barack was expected to go along with the party, and the majority of the time he did. Barack has come under some criticism for voting "present" a lot. Most of those votes came as he was planning and preparing for his future endeavors. When Barack made a plan, he worked it to perfection.

Voting "present" on controversial issues is a common practice among elected officials seeking higher office who don't want to be tied down by a tough vote or two. When Barack voted against my district when we had our altercation, he was running for U.S. Senate. That didn't make him right, and he was forced, by the debate that followed, to try to change his vote. He should have just voted "present" that day.

Barack did have some major accomplishments during his tenure in the Illinois Senate. There are three bills that I consider to be his most important. I am certain there are other bills he passed that were also important, and maybe even more important to him, but these are my three.

The first piece of important legislation he sponsored and passed was the bill to end racial profiling by overzealous police officers. At the time, there were a lot of incidents of Black people being stopped by police for no reason other than the color of their skin. Some police departments in Illinois had unstated, official policies of stopping and detaining Blacks and Latinos. Gay men were also targeted. Two white policemen lost their jobs because they refused to go along with this discriminatory practice, but they sued in court and won.

I had carried the legislation to fight racial profiling for years without success while we Democrats were in the minority. Then, Senator Obama came along and was able to use his negotiating skills to finish the job. Barack was eventually able to get the Fraternal Order of Police, the police union, to support the bill. While the legislation was watered down from my version, it was better than nothing. It didn't take long for me to forget the fact that I had carried the ball 99 yards, and Barack got the call to dive over the top for the touchdown and the glory that comes with it. Getting the legislation passed was all that mattered.

Besides, Barack was on the Judiciary Committee, which deals with criminal justice and is one of the highest-ranking committees in any legislative body. He eventually became chairman of that very powerful group and seemed right at home with the long-winded lawyers there. They love the fine art of expounding on issues and winning every argument, and their meetings lasted forever. And since Barack was very effective on this committee, he got the job done.

After passing the racial profiling legislation, he turned his attention to another big problem in Chicago, forced confessions. The Chicago Police Department had a retired commander named John Burge, who, along with some others in the department, tortured confessions out of people. They used methods that made Guantanamo Bay look like grade school recess. The City of Chicago recently settled some of the lawsuits related to Burge's tactics for a whopping $20 million.

Barack passed legislation that established the policy of videotaping confessions in most serious cases, including murder cases. Illinois had an alarming number of people on death row who were falsely convicted. Many of the false convictions were based on confessions given under serious duress. A cattle prod to the testicles was the most popular method of interrogation employed by the brutal Burge cops, who never went to jail for their crimes.

The third piece of legislation that I consider to be Barack's most important was about campaign finance reform. I have mixed emotions on this legislation because, while well intended, it gives wealthy candidates the advantage. The reforms still allow candidates to contribute as much as they wish from their personal fortunes, while limiting other ways they can raise money for their campaign. I just faced two rich opponents in February of 2008, and it was not easy overcoming their personal wealth, but Barack pushed this bill in order to clean up Illinois politics.

Illinois State Representative Jack Franks, a Democrat and Clinton supporter, has attacked Obama over his high number of "present" votes. While he admitted that he often voted "present" himself because, as an attorney, he had some conflicts of interest from time to time, he failed to mention that Obama is also a lawyer. A "present" vote is sometimes required by law if conflicts of interest may be involved.

Sometimes lawmakers vote "present" because there are some things in a bill you may like and other things that you aren't crazy about. You don't want to vote against the bill, but you can't vote for the bill with the bad amendment on it, so you vote "present." There are also times when you vote "present" because you are working on some part of the bill with the sponsor. I recently voted "present" on a bill that I didn't like because I promised the sponsor I wouldn't vote "no." I owed him a "yes" vote because he voted for my bill to bail out public transportation in Chicago. My friend is from downstate Illinois, and voting "yes" for something in Chicago was not an easy vote for him.

A fairly big deal has been made of Obama's "present" votes, and some of it may be justified, but voting "present" is not to be considered a dereliction of duty.

EIGHT

Mississippi: A Winning Southern Strategy

Over and over again, I heard commentators talking about Barack getting 91 percent of the Black vote when he won the March 11 primary in Mississippi. They repeated his percentage so many times that it became imbedded in my brain. It seemed the message was to brand him as the Black candidate—of course all those Black people voted for him, he's the "Black candidate!" The media completely ignored his sizable white vote in Mississippi.

In Illinois, and all across the country, Obama has been averaging around 85 percent of the Black vote. His appeal among African Americans goes far beyond Mississippi. Every Black precinct I looked at on election night had Barack winning around 88 percent of the Black vote. In my recent race with two challengers, a white female and a bi-racial male, I received around 80 percent of the Black vote. I received about 30 percent of the white vote, and 63 percent of the total vote.

In Mississippi, African Americans made up slightly more than 50 percent of the vote in the Democratic Primary. When you add Barack's strong showing among Blacks with his white vote, you come up with the formula for victory. Obama did not win Mississippi with Black votes alone. In fact, many of the states in his string of eleven straight wins had small Black populations. This fact seemed to be lost on the national media when it came to reporting the results from Mississippi. The results were framed and reported purely along racial lines. Every voter I saw on television, and I watched it all, was Black. Every story started out with the percentage of Black votes that went to Obama, and then we heard a little about the final total. It seemed to me to be another attempt to "Blackenize" Obama.

One commentator led off with something like, "...with a big Black vote in Mississippi, Barack Obama, etc. etc...." Maybe I'm paranoid, but it just sounded like a subliminal reminder of his race to me. Why mention the racial makeup of Mississippi before simply reporting the results? Mississippi gave Obama just a little more of the Black vote than he received in other states.

The beautiful thing about Obama receiving huge votes in Mississippi, South Carolina and across the South is the fact that he can deliver a successful southern strategy for the Democratic Party to recapture the White House this year. I believe we need the South and parts of the West for a Democrat to win, and Barack has shown that he can run well in both of these red state areas—so much so that Barack would almost certainly be the best choice for vice president if he doesn't get the nod for the top spot.

Hillary Clinton, however, would not bring the South or West to a potential Obama/Clinton ticket. In pure long term national politics, the Black candidate is now in play when it comes to the southern strategy for Democrats.

If former Vice-President Al Gore had won his home state of Tennessee in the 2000 election, he would have become the president instead of George W. Bush, and this whole world have been vastly different eight years later. We wouldn't be in Iraq right now, a serious attempt to curb global warming would be well under way, and gas would not be hovering at around four dollars a gallon.

The South and western parts of America are clearly where the presidential race will be won or lost, and this cannot be ignored or conceded to the Republicans. Right now, no other candidate can bring the South to the Democratic Party like Barack Obama. There are a lot of African American voters in the South, and a large turnout by his base could tip several southern states back to the Democratic Party.

And then, on Tuesday, March 11, Rep. Geraldine Ferraro, who ran as Walter Mondale's vice presidential pick during the 1984 presidential election, suggested that Barack has only achieved his status in the presidential campaign because he's Black. She told a newspaper, "If Obama was a white man, he would not be in this position. And if he was a woman (of any color) he would not be in this position. He happens to be very lucky to be who he is. And the country is caught up in the concept."

Wait a minute, Barack Obama is lucky to be Black in America? That is, by far, the most ridiculous thing I have ever heard. I just couldn't believe my ears. Her subsequent follow-ups were just as outrageous—after a barrage of criticism, Ferraro said, "I really think they're attacking me because I'm white."

I once had a great deal of respect for the former congresswoman. I supported her for vice president and was appalled at the prejudiced voices at the time who said she was chosen because she was a woman. What gall she has now to suggest the only thing Obama has going for him is his race and gender. I know and have worked with many politicians of every race, gender, and background. There are good ones and bad ones in every category and combination. Honest and honorable men and women serve side by side with con artists disguised as "elected officials" of every shade, creed, and gender. Race shouldn't be in the race at all.

NINE

Gain the World and Lose Your Soul

It seems odd that I would be writing about the Reverend Wright saga on March 23, Easter Sunday, but what better day to write about redemption, a Black preacher and his parishioner. Barack has been under siege over things Rev. Jeremiah Wright said while in the pulpit.

The pulpit was once the only forum available for the unbridled expression of Black despair and rage. Though many people will say we don't have a grievance with this country, we all know that is not true. In a Black church on any given Sunday, somebody has a testimony involving injustice. America should not underestimate the hurt and pain still felt by Black people to this very day, nor should it turn a blind eye to our current situation in this country. We are still the last hired and the first fired. We still have to listen to and accept bigotry and racial slurs. We still suffer from police brutality, discrimination, and hate, and there most certainly is misunderstanding and distrust on both sides.

Some Black preachers are fiery by their nature—to save poor, desperate people from lives of crime and unhealthy activity takes some energy. There is a style of Black preaching called "whooping" that is designed to get people aroused with spirituality and it often inspires shouting and displays of extreme emotion. I've also learned that every sermon isn't for everybody. I am certain many church members disagree with some things their pastors say. We don't always agree with our church leaders on matters of salvation, sin, finances and politics.

But our heroes have to be perfect with no room for error, and for the first time since meeting him, I feel sorry for Barack. He was forced to repudiate and reprimand his own pastor. This is an extraordinary thing to do in the context of Black church life. How many times has

Reverend Wright preached about something that saved Barack from sin or trouble? How many sermons has he given which gave Barack hope and encouragement? Barack saw his spiritual leader set upon and vilified throughout the media. He had to say something in order to save his campaign, but at what price?

Rev. Jeremiah Wright is a well-respected man of God. The attacks against him have simply gone too far and they have lasted too long. First, there was a campaign to convince people that Barack was a Muslim instead of a friend of Israel. Then there was an attempt to tie him to the Honorable Minister Louis Farrakhan, and now, this attack on Reverend Wright. Barack will probably be completely gray by winter; in fact, he's probably dyeing his hair already. How can you distance yourself from the man that married you to your beloved wife and sleep well at night?

This has to be a personal tragedy for the senator and his wife. The person you look to for moral and spiritual fortitude is very important to a person of faith. More often than not, it's not a choice you make without some yearning from within which moves you to follow that person. Their ability to nourish your soul—not their personal politics—is what matters most.

I'm certain Reverend Wright has forgiven Barack, if he feels it's necessary. He understands politics and how nasty the game can get. I'm sure he has also prayed for his accusers. Love, forgiveness, compassion, and redemption are all part of the Black Church doctrine. I hope when he becomes president, Barack will still attend Trinity. He gave a great speech qualifying his positions on race and tolerance, and I sincerely hope Americans listened with an open mind. Barack is not prejudiced in any way.

I was having a long conversation with three friends of mine, one is Black, one is white, and one is Hispanic. They all worked on my campaign and all are Obama supporters. Things were said that screamed to be in this book and are pertinent to the dilemma we Democrats find ourselves in.

The first thing that caught me off guard was that my Black friend felt that Barack should quit his church. I asked my friend, a devout Christian, if he would abandon his pastor and he said he would not, but that Barack should. We discussed this point for a very long time because I couldn't disagree more. My white friend agreed with my Black buddy on this issue. Our Latino friend remained quiet as if not wanting to get in the middle of this disagreement.

The discussion then turned to the subject of a joint ticket—Obama/Clinton. Immediately, my Black friend said, "Hell no!" I was thrown for a loop. He went on to say that Barack should never choose Hillary Clinton as his vice president after having had to defend himself from her vicious attacks. He didn't want to even consider an Obama/Clinton ticket and promised to vote for McCain if such a thing came to pass. He swore that most of his friends have said the same thing.

This was coming from a very intelligent man. My friend is a middle-class, politically savvy guy, so his feelings caused me great pause. I tried to explain the self-destructive nature of taking such drastic action, but practically got my head chewed off. Our white friend also attempted to calm our buddy's wrath to no avail. My attempts to change the subject were fruitless. I explained how politicians may get together before the convention and cut a deal for either the dream or nightmare ticket. This seemed to anger my friend even more, and he demanded that the super delegates follow the will of the people. He didn't want to see Hillary Clinton anywhere near Barack Obama.

My buddy told us the story of how one of his old street buddies was now watching CNN everyday for political updates instead of his usual diet of *Flavor of Love*. He said people's lives have been changed because of Obama's run for the White House, and they simply are not going to accept anything less than the presidency.

I gave up and found a nice way to head home before all of our years of friendship were ruined over two politicians—make that three. My friend also ranted and raved about Bill Clinton being an obstructionist in any Obama/Clinton White House. It was definitely time to run for cover, but my buddy represents a dangerous, growing sentiment in the Black community. The Republicans must be laughing all the way to the bank.

I decided that perhaps I better stop defending Hillary Clinton and just look out for number one, me. I wondered how many other elected officials of all colors are coming to this conclusion, because if

Black people stay at home or split their ballot in the November general election, all of the local Democrats in tight races will be jeopardized. The old saying that "all politics is local" may not apply this year, and the outcome could be devastating. My friend and many, many others seem determined to cut off their nose to spite their face. The idea of refusing to support Hillary Clinton if she should win the nomination is much more prevalent than I thought.

At this point, I am extremely worried. The media reported that American deaths in Iraq have topped 4,000. How much more blood will we sacrifice for this conflict? I don't want to see the war continue. I don't want gas to be over four dollars a gallon. I don't want foreclosures to continue to skyrocket. Democrats must support whichever candidate wins the nomination over John McCain.

When I turned on the 10 o'clock news that evening, there stood the woman I was just staunchly defending to my friends, committing a cardinal sin. Senator Clinton was berating Barack for not quitting his church. I wanted to jump though the screen and shout, "Enough all ready! Let it go!" I wondered who Hillary's Black advisors were. Does she have anyone telling her truth, or is she refusing to listen to their counsel?

It will seriously damage her efforts to demand that Obama flee his pastor and congregation. Black church folks and senior citizens vote more than any other segment of African Americans. The Clintons have been around Black churches for a very long time. Even when former President Clinton was facing impeachment, his support in the Black community stayed strong. In fact, it actually rose in strength and ferocity.

The same dynamic is at work as it relates to Barack Obama. Both he and Rev. Jeremiah Wright are rising to heroic proportions among most Black people because of the controversy. "Blackenizing" Barack has clearly worked, and it may win Hillary the nomination, but it will cost her the ultimate goal. She will never become the president. Blacks are getting very ugly towards her and Bill, the "First Black President," and that is very unfortunate.

To win at any cost is a travesty. The Clintons need to also consider the pain and anguish they are causing all the people who loved and respected them more than anyone else.

The news is reporting that there have been numerous death threats on Reverend Wright's life. What's new? Anybody remember Dr. Martin Luther King Jr.? Throughout history, the Black pastor has come under attack. In my opinion Dr. King died because some misguided people considered him to be anti-American for things he said in his sermons. Now another prominent Black minister is in trouble over how he stated some things.

Black pain is often expressed on Sundays as we pray for justice, equal opportunity, and God's mercy and grace. Often it seems our prayers are not heard and the pastor has to give us hope and gird up our faith. We cry out and nobody hears but our pastors. We bury our young, and who cries with us, our pastors. We can't pay our bills or send our children to college, and who helps us? The Black pastor, the keeper of the flock, the good shepherd. The good shepherd absorbs the pain of his flock, shows sympathy and compassion and then directs them to a way to find peace within.

One reporter wrote about the members of the press who hovered around Trinity United Church of Christ expecting some sort of rebellion against Reverend Wright. It's amazing what little respect we are given. He wrote about how they went from person to person seeking just one negative comment and how surprised they were that none was forthcoming. Has Reverend Wright cast some spell on these poor unsuspecting souls? Could the entire congregation be filled with ungrateful, anti-American sinners? Maybe they just know and love their pastor.

Barack should not allow this character assassination to ruin his relationship with the people who consider him their brother in Christ. I guess we've officially entered the "Anything to Stop Obama" phase of the campaign. America is still not ready for a Black president and it may never be ready for one.

The dark, grainy photos and drawings of Barack will surely hit the public eye soon. Some spin doctor is working on that just as sure as gas prices will continue to rise. I've had it done to me; my opponent used images that darkened my face and made me look so ominous that if I didn't know me, I would have been afraid of myself! Get ready for the really Black Barack.

On March 30, station after station is reporting that 28 percent of Hillary supporters say they won't vote for Obama, and 18 percent of Obama supporters told pollsters they won't vote for Clinton, whichever one should win the nomination. So, what's really going on? I really can't figure out the Clinton supporters. For the most part, Obama has taken the high road and has not attacked Senator Clinton on any personal issues.

I've watched most of the debates, I've read everything related to politics I can get my hands on, and I never miss the news on television, but I can't recall Barack ever saying anything about Hillary negative enough to bring about that much resentment from her supporters. Both camps have traded barbs, but normally the candidates remain above the fray. This has not been the case this time, and with former President Bill Clinton leading the way, it's almost two against one. Poor Barack is caught in the crossfire and he never fired a shot.

We must examine the reasons behind this very large, and apparently mean-spirited, anti-Obama backlash. Is the Democratic Party, which has been seen as the answer to Black people's problems, a racist party? Or is gender the issue?

The problem here is that Black people did not, and currently are not, the cause of gender bias or discrimination in America. When I listen to Geraldine Ferraro and activists for women's rights who are supporting Hillary Clinton say, "It's our turn!" it seems that many of them are expressing outrage that Obama is somehow stealing what belongs to a woman, and as a result, he is anti-female. At the very least, they are clearly placing a terrible injustice in this country at the feet of another of America's victims, the Black man.

We share the common scars of discrimination, disrespect, and the glass ceiling. The civil rights movement and women's rights movement have always been and are still intertwined. The history of our mutual support screams from our past. The gains we earned through our coordinated efforts beg us to cease and desist from this insanity. Those great American heroes who died in Iraq are not separated by gender or race when the body bags come home. With the problems we face as Americans today, we cannot afford to further divide this country.

I should have gone to bed, or at least turned off the television, but I ended up watching the late night news and the early morning talk shows. Senator John McCain said some odd things and made a few gaffes, but the Democratic infighting dominated the news. Even the Republicans who don't like McCain are extremely happy right now. I spoke with a few Republicans I serve with, and they all expressed joy at being let back in the game due to the infighting. Somebody needs to be benched for the good of the team. I believe every state should have their voice, but soon a decision must be made so the healing process can begin. Politicians will get over it, but many of the true believers will be harmed for life.

Trust me people, these two senators and powerful families will probably get together and slice up a big hog while you suicidal supporters will be left out. You will look up at your TV, and there they will stand, Barack and Hillary, hand-in-hand, smiling and kissing like they just got married. The praise they will lavish on each other will be over the top.

Remember, these are professional talkers. And, of course, when the questions come from the tough press corps over things he said and she said, the spin doctors would have them ready with the right response. So, while you are contemplating doing great bodily harm to someone on the other side, the back channels between the campaigns may be already open. The possibility of a Dream Ticket of the two could end up as your sweetest reality, or worst nightmare. I guess it all depends on which name is on top.

TEN

The Speech of a Lifetime

On March 18 in Philadelphia, Barack made his historic speech on race in answer to the attacks on remarks made by his pastor, Rev. Jeremiah Wright. Barack had to confront demons from America's past that refuse to go away: slavery, slave masters, love, hate, pride and shame—all had to be dissected and examined like never before. The things at stake made this the most important speech in modern American history. When Rev. Jesse Jackson ran for president he dealt with this thorny issue, but times were different then, and he never had a real chance of winning, so he had less to lose. Barack Obama was the front-runner when he was forced by the words of others to deal head on with the issue he wished to avoid more than any other. In an election where race was the determining factor, he was a sure loser—with his black skin.

Yet, here it was front and center. No matter how he couched it, the question of race relations in America was touchy and divisive. White people simply don't want to hear it. They consider things that still trouble Black people as it relates to our treatment in this country as unwarranted gripes. The "Angry Black Man" could never be elected president in America, so somehow Barack had to hide his pain—and he was cool as ever. He delivered a serious lengthy speech on race without coming across as being too resentful of our diverse nation. Many Black leaders would have failed at this assignment—including yours truly. I tend to get emotional when I think about the "good old days." It wasn't so good for my family in the late 1950s and early 1960s.

When I was a troubled young teenager being chased by the big four, a mean group of police in Chicago, I saw racism up close and in person, and it was not pretty. When Black Panther leader Fred Hampton and Mark Clark were killed—a few blocks from where I live right now, my high school marched to the house on Monroe—under the raised hooves of frightened horses carrying billy club-swinging police in riot gear. We walked proudly as they called us niggers and tried to provoke us. My sister Shebeta fainted when we saw the bullet holes in the walls which screamed out "Massacre!" We dared to demand justice.

The stench of death filled my teenage lungs, and the bloodstained walls ripped at my soul—guaranteeing me vivid nightmares for quite some time. It was a good thing that Barack Obama was a young child at that time and never was forced to witness such a morbid disaster. When Dr. King was killed and raging fires engulfed Chicago's West Side, expressing the rage of a hopeless people, I was right smack dab in the middle. My mother, Olivia, did everything she could to keep my brother Gerome and me in the house, but we snuck out the back door and ran up to Pulaski were I tried to stop a crazed mob from burning down my favorite sixth grade teacher's store. I'll never forget Gee pulling me out of the way of the National Guard's jeep, which flew past my 70-pound frame as they chased after the looters who ignored my pleas to spare my white teacher from Bryant Elementary, Mr. Richie's store.

If he heard about Chicago's Mayor Richard J. Daley's orders to shoot to kill, Barack was too young to understand why he gave that order, or even why his people were acting so ugly. Perhaps this reality made it easier for Barack to make his life-altering speech without crying or screaming out in pain. He also did not see the white victims of the race riots, like my teacher and those who died simply because they were at the wrong place at the wrong time. My heart wept for both sides of Obama's lineage, whose blood flowed in the streets though out America.

Even though Barack passed the bill to end racial profiling in the state of Illinois, he admitted it never happened to him. I know that made it easier for him to compromise on that bill, just like being a victim of unwarranted stops by police made it harder for me to seek common ground. Because of his life experiences Barack was able to make the compromises needed between Blacks and whites on race related problems to move America forward. In his speech he forced us to face up to the past, exorcise those demons and look to the future. His delivery was romantic, his words reassuring, and his tone was firm yet conciliatory. I knew it was going to be well received by every race, creed and color. He released white people from any guilt they may have inherited and assigned it to a history long passed away. He also freed Black people from the shame of being captives and the self-hate that came with it.

His sense of hope penetrated the airwaves and brought peace to those who still struggled with the past. A new era was born and change was within reach. We could believe again, hope again, and not just pray to God and wait for the day to come because this was that day America had been waiting for.

ELEVEN

The Mexican Standoff: Why Are Latinos Voting for Hillary and Not Obama?

On March 21, 2008, Governor Bill Richardson from the state of New Mexico, and the nation's only Hispanic governor, endorsed Barack. The timing couldn't have been better for Obama, who has been under attack because of Reverend Wright. In addition, Governor Richardson is a super delegate and a former member of Bill Clinton's administration. I'm certain Hillary Clinton is pondering that old political saying, "There are no permanent friends or enemies, just permanent interests." I'm not calling Richardson's endorsement a betrayal of the Clintons, but I'd be surprised if they don't consider it one.

I must admit I was a little surprised because Latinos across America have favored Hillary Clinton, especially Mexican Americans. Even here in Illinois, Obama lost the Latino vote to her in the February 5 Super Tuesday election in Illinois. I believe she even did better than Governor Richardson himself with Hispanics in the primaries before he dropped out of the race. I thought that as the first viable Latino to run for president, he would do much better with this important segment of the Democratic Party.

It seemed to me that the governor did not run as the Great Latino Hope, although everybody knew of his proud Mexican heritage. But I noticed that he was not placed under the media and public microscope as "the first Latino" presidential candidate like Obama was

57

as "the first viable Black" presidential candidate. This was evident long before Barack became the front-runner. There is still some reluctance to accept Black people as leaders in America, even today. Of course, I would love to be proven wrong on this.

Now, the question is, will Richardson's endorsement translate into votes for Obama? I believe it may only have a small effect because Latinos weren't voting for the governor when he himself was a candidate. I believe most will still support Senator Clinton. The sad thing about this reality is the fact that Obama has offered a much more progressive agenda for Latinos.

On the issue of immigration, Obama has been supportive of Hispanic demands and the path to citizenship. While in Springfield, Obama always was open to their agenda. In fact, the Black Caucus is the one group from which Latinos have generally received unconditional support. In the future, however, that blind support may be in jeopardy. The lack of mutual support by our fellow minorities is a body blow to African American legislators. In Illinois, the relationship between Black and brown has clearly deteriorated, and major pieces of their agenda have stalled.

An example of this is their desire to get drivers licenses even if they are undocumented immigrants. At one time, this legislation was on the verge of passing and becoming law in Illinois. The main supporters were Blacks from the Chicago—seven solid votes. Now the bill isn't even being called. Downstate, white Democrats and all of Illinois' Republican legislators are against it. Republicans are also advancing a bill that would deny health care to undocumented children. Latino leaders are depending on Black legislators to kill the bill, but so far it is moving forward. This lack of mutual support is a very unfortunate development that will be detrimental to both groups. I have always pushed joint meetings between the two caucuses, but to no avail. There is a real schism between us, and to ignore it is to feed into it.

I spoke with a very prominent Mexican American state senator about our dilemma. My colleague was bluntly honest with me. He explained how his people come to America seeking a better life. They come here for economic reasons and to pursue the American Dream. They want to assimilate with white people, not Black people. He asked me if Mexicans move into the Black community when they come here, and I had to admit they do not. I appreciated his honest open airing of his views because such honesty is so rare to hear in politics.

Bill Richardson is America's only Hispanic governor. I hope his endorsement can bridge this growing divide. If he had endorsed Obama before the Texas primary, the race could have been over, but I guess it's better late than never. Unfortunately for Barack, even with Governor Richardson's support, he is losing to Hillary Clinton in the polls in Puerto Rico. This shows that the disconnect between Blacks and Latinos goes beyond the Mexican immigrant community.

TWELVE

Super Delegates/Super Dilemma

My, my, what a mess we've spun. We Democrats find ourselves in a no-win situation. If we dump Obama and choose Clinton, Black and independent voters will be outraged. If we choose Barack over Hillary, some women will be turned off. If either constituency abandons the party, we will keep a Republican president and the war will continue as John McCain has said, for maybe 100 more years. I am not a super delegate, but I feel their pain. They must be watching this sad saga with the Maalox nearby.

Poor Howard Dean, what in the world can he do about the debacles in Michigan and Florida? The Democratic National Committee (DNC) stripped both states of their delegates as punishment for holding their primaries too early. Barack's name wasn't even on the ballot in Michigan, which Hillary won, and now the governors of those states are screaming for their delegates to be put back in the game somehow.

As Chairman of the DNC, I guess Dean can do several things: he can sit on his hands and do nothing, and embrace the eventual nominee. He could demand and work towards re-votes in Florida and Michigan and anger Obama's people. Or, he can demand that all of the super delegates express their sentiments now and end the carnage.

The Clinton camp has been accused of being engaged in a whispering campaign against Obama with the super delegates. Accused? Hell, that's par for the course in politics! Whispers, lies and innuendo are normal functions during a heated election, and sometimes the dust lingers long after the voters have decided the outcome. Senator Clinton's backroom operators are spreading the word that, in their opinion, Barack can't win. They claim to have negative secrets that will surely come out in a general election. In cases like this, the gossipers never tell you the secret they have, they ask you to trust them.

Unfortunately for Obama and the people of this country, lies are often believed. I know super delegates from both campaigns, and they all are complaining about the level of bitterness between the warring factions. Obama's campaign claims they are not going to get involved in this nasty little whispering attack. I would be fighting back with similar tactics, but I take them at their word. These kinds of nasty tactics can, and often do, turn on the accusers. Sometimes people get tired of all the negativity. Elected officials and super delegates also understand that it is hard to take back negative things that you said in a primary because the Republicans will use those things in the general election.

THIRTEEN

Real Change or Chump Change?

Recently the handlers of Hillary Clinton have gone overboard. They are trying to paint Obama as some kind of crazy radical instead of an agent of reasonable change. The attempts to tarnish Barack with the words of his pastor have worked. I would laugh if it was funny, but it's not. The Barack Obama I know is far from radical or militant. Honestly, he wasn't even considered a seriously aggressive community activist.

I can't recall Barack ever being at any police brutality meeting or rally. There have been some very questionable police shootings in Chicago, and I don't know one in which the senator joined in the protest. We had a minority contract scandal involving Mayor Daley's administration where white contractors were getting the bulk of funds that had been set aside for minority contractors. Politicians like me and Congressman Jesse Jackson Jr. demanded reform, but not Barack. He never said a word. He showed that he knows how to go along to get along.

I am not suggesting that he doesn't fight these things quietly behind the scenes. I'm sure he does, but true activism is quite visible. By its nature, it challenges the system and does so boldly and without fear. Obama is not even a minor threat to the status quo. He will intelligently think all issues through and unite this divided country of ours.

If you look at the major issues espoused by the senator, you will not find anything radical or shocking—especially about the plight of Black people in America. He even gave a speech in which he basically said, "Pull yourself up by your own bootstraps." There were serious calls for Senator Obama to say something—anything—about the Jena 6, but in political electability terms, he wisely avoided the conflict and only issued a mild statement. He certainly didn't join this nation's civil rights leaders in Jena.

Now, it would be radical if Obama were pushing for reparations for African Americans. I personally believe this country should pay reparations for the forced enslavement of Black people, but it's not a popular idea with mainstream America, so it's not on the agenda. Actually, I don't consider it radical; I simply think it would be justice. If we were any other race, I believe the history of this country proves we would have gotten our just due a long time ago. Reparations would be real "change." Anything less is just more of the same to me.

Real change would be something similar to what Congressman Danny Davis of Illinois just accomplished. He passed a bill that gives $326 million to an ex-offender program and got President Bush to sign it. Working to keep people from going back to jail instead of concentrating on incarceration is real change, not chump change. Many people are looking for Obama to talk about programs like these, not rolling back affirmative action. This is not to suggest that he doesn't care about affirmative action or equal opportunity—I'm just certain Barack's handlers have told him to stay away from such subjects if he wants to become the next President of these United States.

Poor whites and other disadvantaged people are diluting the very premise on which affirmation action was established by President Richard Nixon. But, Barack has made it clear that, if elected president, he would level the playing field, and Black people would not be the only ones getting affirmative action. To have a Black hero espousing the very idea that Blacks and other minorities have an advantage because of affirmative action is ludicrous. I'm writing this chapter so my people can prepare themselves for some possible mind-boggling actions from our first Black president. If he can talk against affirmative action on national TV and get a pass, we are in serious trouble.

In Chicago this weekend, 32 young people were shot. Most of them were Black and the rest were Latino. The victims and the shooters are poor high school students. People came on TV proposing another study to discover and understand the reasons. Why not just dust off the numerous old studies and apply the knowledge they contain, then use the money saved to start jobs programs for these troubled youth. Build some alternative schools for these children and allow them to re-enroll instead of making them permanent dropouts.

There are no job programs or high school re-entry programs like there were at one time. Today, if a child drops out of school and reaches the age of 19, they can't get back in—society just throws them away. These children feel abandoned, unloved and despised—no wonder they turn to the street where they are accepted and given comfort. Gangsters, rappers and music videos control our children's mindset. Most of the lyrics on hip-hop radio promote a thug lifestyle as the only way out of the ghetto, unless you can run for a long touchdown or shoot a basketball.

A recent study names drug sales and gang activity as the main causes of violence in urban America. If we gave people economic opportunities like the fat cats receive, many of our troubled youth could turn their lives around. We had a minority participation program here in Chicago that had to be discontinued because of fraud by white men in Mayor Daley's administration and Obama remained silent.

It would be nice to hear the senator speak to the problems these young people face. They expect so much from him, as does the entire hip-hop generation that is fueling his candidacy. I repeat, 32 young people were shot on a single weekend. We need real solutions, real change, not just a pretty face. I call it like I see it, especially when it involves life and death.

FOURTEEN

Dream Ticket or a Nightmare?

I can dream can't I? After a long day and an even longer night, I had a dream about the perfect ticket. Barack was being sworn in as president, and Hillary Clinton was being given the oath of office as vice president. I didn't want to let go of this wistful imagining, but unfortunately, the phone rang and my dream turned into a nightmare. A friend was ranting about something Senator Clinton had said and couldn't wait for a decent hour. I kindly wrangled my way off the phone and attempted to restore my wonderful dream, but to no avail. I lay on my pillow and allowed myself to dwell on the illusion of Democratic unity. The Dream Team was the perfect ending, and it really didn't matter which candidate was on top. Either way, we would make historic leaps forward here in America.

I was convinced that the teaming of Obama and Clinton was the perfect political marriage. I wondered if the needs of the people came before their personal dreams, wishes and desires. I was starting to have my doubts, especially about Hillary. She has decided to go so negative against Barack, and the ramifications are enormous. People I know who once loved her and hung on her every word are close to actual hatred. Many of the strongest Black Clinton supporters I've ever known are cursing the day they voted for the "First Black President" and they no longer affectionately call Bill Clinton by that title. They're calling him something much worse as he seems to demean Barack at every step as he continues on the stump campaigning for his wife.

My argument for patience is falling on deaf ears. Things are really going south, and I am beginning to wonder if either candidate will survive this bumpy road to the White House. My wonderful dream is turning into a nightmare!

FIFTEEN

The Art of War

The Comeback Kid had a bad week, but she is well versed in the art of war. On April 8 things heated up. Senator Clinton had to let go of her main campaign strategist, Mark Penn. Penn was a paid staff member on the Clinton team who got caught up in a deal involving trade with Columbia. Organized labor has accused the Columbian government of brutalizing workers seeking to unionize. Penn is also a consultant, and his company met with the Columbians over this agreement.

The appearance is what hurts. Penn did nothing wrong, but Senator Clinton is on record against this particular Free Trade Deal. She is also under fire over her previous support of the Free Trade Agreement pushed by her husband, President Clinton. She denies she ever spoke in favor of it, but they are showing tapes of her doing just that, and the Teamsters are supporting Obama, partly because of the trade agreement, which hurt American workers.

This Penn/union issue will hurt Hillary in Pennsylvania, and longtime consultant Dick Morris now predicts she may lose there. If she does, it is all over—the fat lady will have sung. I'm not ready to declare Pennsylvania for Obama just yet, but if Hillary doesn't stop the bleeding soon, the state might swing Obama's way. The American people get nervous when they hear that lobbyists are paid campaign strategists because of potential conflicts of interest. Some fear they are too close to the candidate and may put other interests ahead of America's best interest. Don't get me wrong; I take contributions from lobbyists and I recognize their role as spelled out in our constitution. The people have the right to petition their government and advocate for issues, but when the lobbyists also run campaigns, things can get tricky.

Mark Penn is still around the Clinton campaign, and they say he is still trying to raise money behind the scenes. Dick Morris said last night on *Hannity and Colmes* on Fox TV, that the Clinton camp would be satisfied if Obama just retired Hillary Clinton's $20 million campaign debt, much of which was owed to her husband.

The Pennsylvania primary is only two weeks away, and I know both candidates are growing weary; it has been a long, tough road. If you look into their faces, you can see the strain that rough and tumble elections have on the mind, spirit, and soul. The forced smiles when you are exhausted and long speeches in distant places take their toll. I'll be glad when it's over, and I'm not either one of them. In my own election this year, I was running unopposed until this morning. But now the Republicans have appointed some unknown against me for the general election, so I need to step up and handle my own campaign.

The intensity of this battle is starting to cast doubt on the possibility of a Dream Ticket. The animosity may have become too bitter to repair enough for Barack and Hillary to be able to team up. I still think it would be good for Barack to select Hillary as his running mate. In a year of change, who would be a better choice? Certainly not a white male. Governor Bill Richardson would be a bold and daring choice, but I believe two racial minorities running together would be doomed.

I do not believe the Mark Penn incident is enough to make Clinton damaged goods, and she remains attractive as a running mate. She has a strong following of dedicated people who may stay home if she is not on the ticket. Both candidates' supporters will still come out and vote if the two leaders team up, despite the current sentiments that both groups have expressed.

On April 12, the conclusion of this battle was pushed until after Indiana and North Carolina. Many pundits predicted the end of Hillary when the Mark Penn incident was followed by Bill Clinton reviving the false sniper fire in Bosnia story. He blamed it on his wife's age and campaign fatigue. This totally undermined her 3 a.m. phone call ads against Obama. Clinton quickly chastised her husband, but the damage was done. Two bad stories about her were in the news at the same time.

Things could not have been any better for Barack, and most polls in Pennsylvania suddenly showed him closing fast. He was also holding a huge lead in cash on hand and was outspending Hillary by three to one there. But, just when it seemed the Obama nomination was close at hand, another snafu by Barack occurred—the slight miscue in San Francisco. Obama was at a private fundraiser for wealthy supporters when he attempted to explain his lack of strong support in some small towns. Being among friends, he tried to explain how people are angry about the economy and seek refuge in odd ways. Barack said that "bitter" small-town Americans "cling to guns and religion" to deal with their frustrations.

His use of the word "bitter" was taken way out of context. The vast majority of the American people say this country of ours is headed in the wrong direction. We are clearly angry and looking for answers. Now, "bitter" may have been too strong a word, but there is no denying our anxiety. Look at President Bush's extremely low approval ratings. Some people probably are bitter about losing their jobs to overseas workers, losing their homes to foreclosure, and paying outrageous prices for gasoline.

How bad must things get before people get upset or bitter? One thing for sure—Americans in small towns are feeling the same crunch as those in the big cities; we are all suffering together. Stating the obvious should not derail Obama's train, but you can't tell that to Clinton's camp. They have pounced on this comment with the ferocity of a mad pit bull. Hillary herself was just on television implying that Barack is everything from an elitist to an arrogant, pompous, insensitive jerk. I know she wants to win, and she may be desperate, but this is over the top.

My dreams of a unity ticket are being blown away by her relentless attacks. How can any Black man in America be an elitist and look down on anybody in this country? It's an outrageous charge! Obama can graduate from Harvard, Yale, or Princeton, and go on to become the president, yet he will still be looked down upon by some people in this country. There are people in America who will still call him "boy" and openly disrespect his presidency.

Barack's subsequent apologies and clarifications seemed to be falling on deaf ears in the media, but I have yet to hear any of the

Sunday morning pundits deny that we Americans are, in fact, upset. The vast majority of Americans have begun to resent the war, and we resent having been lied to. Bush never found any weapons of mass destruction. Our second excuse for invading Iraq—Saddam Hussein—has been prosecuted and executed, and his sons have also been killed. We found over a billion dollars in cash in various bunkers, Halliburton is making a fortune in no-bid contracts, and gas is almost four dollars a gallon.

People know that both President Bush and Vice President Cheney are oil executives who benefit from high gas prices. As soon as they leave office, watch who comes calling on them with a delayed compensation package or lucrative offer. It won't be small town America or middle-class America. In fact, we may not have a middle class by then. Two Americas are emerging as I write this sad saga, the extremely rich and the very poor. People who own lots of stock in big oil companies are enjoying record profits, and people wealthy enough to purchase foreclosed properties are getting bargains. The rich get richer, the poor get poorer, and the middle class gets squeezed towards the bottom. So, if "bitter" is too strong a word, maybe "pissed off" will suffice.

I'm sorry to say my love for Hillary Clinton and my favorite president of all time is starting to die a slow, but certain death as they continue this assault on Barack. This is madness, insanity, and self-mutilation. The Democratic Party is headed for defeat and everyone in America will pay the price. If this infighting does not come to an end, Senator John McCain will win the presidency. If that happens, I predict we will invade Iran, gas will top five dollars a gallon across the country, and foreclosures will soar beyond repair.

Real human tragedy awaits us and we may as well prepare ourselves. This war is the reason we can't get the economy back on track. Every disposable dollar is being spent on this continual cycle of death. Can you imagine where we would be if we had spent four trillion dollars on fixing America instead of Iraq? We want a president who will put Americans first!

I am not surprised to hear people who get upset over the enormous amounts of money we send to other counties while our own infrastructure crumbles. If I sound bitter, then maybe Barack Obama was talking about me.

April 18, 2008, the Pennsylvania primary is only four days away, and it is clear that it will only continue the slow death of the Democratic Party on the national level. Senator Clinton will win that primary and continue her campaign of mass destruction.

The Clinton camp has picked at Obama's slightest defects like an infection on a baby's bottom. Most Blacks feel the Clinton campaign has spread lies, fanned the flames of racism, and even broadened old misunderstandings with no regard to the long-term effect on the Democratic Party. Her campaign is operating like a virus that seeks to weaken the body, destroy the victim and then attach itself to another innocent bystander.

It's beginning to seem like it's "we win or we all lose" with them. The only people happy are Senator John McCain and the war mongering industrial complex, which still exists in America. The Clintons have been so fixated on bloodying up Obama they can't see the damage they are causing to themselves. To win at all cost is a sure way to lose and a selfish way to go about it. The wounds inflicted upon Barack are being felt by people of every race. I would expect this kind of ruthless selfishness from the Republican right wing, but not the family once so highly revered by the Black community.

The final primary debate was held on April 16, leading up to the Pennsylvania primary on April 22. The first half-hour must have seemed like an earthquake aftershock to Barack as both commentators for ABC attacked him relentlessly over issues pushed by Hillary's spin doctors and gossip spreaders. The moderators, Charlie Gibson and George Stephanopoulos may as well have been on her payroll. It was clearly a planned and well-coordinated assault by two men with great press credentials and mounds of respect. Who better to cause a political earthquake than two supposedly unbiased television icons?

I couldn't help but wonder if it was just an attempt at raising the ratings or simply bad television. In this day and age, I also had to wonder if something more sinister was going on. Either way I'm sure Barack learned a lesson or two from the one-sided and mostly lame questions such as: "Why doesn't he wear an American flag lapel pin?" I'm about to watch one of the commentators of the vicious debate the other night. One of my favorite Sunday morning talk programs is *This*

Week with George Stephanopoulos. One of his topics is the debate over the debate. Many major news outlets were very critical of ABC and the moderators over the lack of real substance in the candidates' debate and the harsh grilling of only one candidate, Barack Obama. The guest panel on *This Week* were kind to George and Charles Gibson, the other questioner, but it was clear that the public missed a wonderful opportunity to learn more about the policies of the two contenders during the debate.

No wonder this election may turn on who can drink the most beer or bowl over 100. On the national scene, some newscasters are making more hoopla over candidates chugging one down than their agendas. Hoisting a beer to gain some votes is the theme of the day. The spin doctors have convinced the candidates that this will endear them to the average voters. As the campaigns swing to southern states, support for gun ownership rights is also in vogue, even as violence spirals out of control in Chicago and all across America. It will be a good day when the campaigns can get to the business of solving America's problems.

Tomorrow is the Pennsylvania primary and the real topics are not being discussed. The last poll I saw was on how beer drinkers, gun owners and bowlers were planning to vote. Well, let me say that I have owned guns, drank my share, and bowl a decent score, so I ain't hating. But, today with gas at four bucks a gallon, it's the economy stupid! The moderators should have pounded Obama and Clinton about their plans to get us out of this mess instead of spending over half the debate on slips of the lips. How about a discussion on how they intend to reduce the violence in our community? Americans are fighting to keep homes out of foreclosure, and all they can ask about is Reverend Wright and the definition of the word "bitter."

We are mired in the murky waters of two wars, and the big questions were about an old relic from the Vietnam era that had been long forgotten by most of us. Bill Ayers of the Weather Underground did some terrible things as a '60s radical, but I have to ask, how old is this 1960s hippy today, damn near 70? Has he changed, or is he online trying to contact Osama bin Laden even as we speak? I would have appreciated a lengthy discussion about today's conflicts and today's active terrorists. Bill Ayers is a quiet grandpa now, and Barack was eight years old when Ayers was a young militant, as were many other youths of his day.

The polls open in the Keystone State in the morning, and not a minute too soon. Most recent polls in Pennsylvania have Hillary Clinton up by five to seven points, but I believe she will only win by six points, and maybe as few as four points. As long as Obama does not get blown away, things will be just fine.

It will take a 10-point victory or more for Clinton to make any real gain in the delegate count. One of the reasons I believe the vote will be close is Senator Clinton's very high negative rating of 54 percent. Obama's negative rating has also gone up, but is at only 39 percent. It seems the negative campaigns have muddied up both candidates, but most of the backlash has fallen on Hillary, not Barack. Negative attacks can backfire on a candidate, and it's beginning to look as if that is what is happening.

The nightly news anchors have just gone off, and I can breathe again. On just about every channel they continued to mention that Obama was outspending Clinton by two to one. They seemed amazed that he still has such a large amount of cash on hand while she is in debt. It's as if they continue to overlook the record number of small donors who continue to give what little they have to his campaign. These small donors are better than the big rich donors because they are far more numerous, committed and determined. They also represent a much larger pool of new voters for the recipient of their hard earned dollars. Obama has also raised more money over the Internet than any candidate in history. He is still predicted to lose tomorrow to Clinton in Pennsylvania, but let's look at what a loss actually means for Obama in this key race.

Since Pennsylvania is only 10 percent Black, if Obama gets 47 percent of the popular vote, he has done well. This will prove that he can win in a big state with a small Black population, like he did in Iowa and other small states. If he does better than 47 percent, his delegate lead will hardly slip at all. A five point or less win for Clinton is a draw in most minds. In addition, with this election distributing delegates according to proportional representation and not winner take all, Obama will just about break even. Considering the pure hell of the last

30 days, that's not bad at all. He could end this nightmare on May 6 in Indiana and North Carolina by taking both states.

SIXTEEN

The Comeback Kid, Again!

Once again, Senator Hillary Rodham Clinton has shown amazing resilience. She won Pennsylvania by a wide margin. A 10-point Clinton victory has given her momentum. There is no doubt about it. The final percentages were Clinton at 55 percent to Obama's 45 percent. The big money began to role in immediately and Clinton raised $3 million the night of her victory.

Momentum can be a powerful thing, and an opponent's momentum needs to be shut down as soon as possible. Unfortunately, during a campaign, you can't call a timeout like you can in sports. The days and rallies and speeches are going to keep on coming, and that calendar will turn. The Obama campaign is most certainly well aware of this, so they will not panic. They should tip their hat to Senator Clinton, as I now do, and then go out and fight to end this thing. Sometimes you simply have to fight. People will sometimes take kindness for weakness, and I've heard people suggest that Barack is not tough enough.

Not Black enough, not white enough, and now not tough enough—that is another dilemma. If Barack goes as negative on Hillary, as she has gone on him, will it cause him to lose his chance in the general election? That is the question. He certainly can't run out the clock because Indiana and North Carolina are looming. Not to mention Guam, with its now very important three delegates. Guam's primary is May 3, to be followed by North Carolina and Indiana three days later.

Several months ago, I was with some lawmakers from Indiana, and they thought this race would be all over by the time it reached their state. Now the eyes of the world are on Indiana. The world is also watching Barack Obama. They know Hillary is tough, they have seen her under fire and on the attack. She has done battle and she has proven to be ready on the first day. I believe Barack is ready too, but I think his handlers are telling him to be kinder and gentler.

Hell, people want a fighter! The entrenched powers in our country are not going to just hand that power over to Barack Obama or Hillary Clinton. This general election is going to be of epic proportions—and very nasty. But, if the Obama campaign fires back at Clinton, will white women be offended? Will she be able to play the victim if things get brutal? Barack must decide. If it were me, I would fight back with everything I had.

Barack is looking a little worse for the wear, and that's natural. Campaigns can suck the life out of anyone, and this one has to be draining, not just for the candidate, but for the entire Obama family.

All I wanted to do was order breakfast to go, sip down my coffee and quietly read the paper. Instead there I was in a lively discussion about Rev. Jeremiah Wright. The diner's opinions varied as much as Miss Edna's menu at the legendary West Side of Chicago restaurant. It's April 25, and Reverend Wright is back in the news. He defended himself last night on Bill Moyers show like the seasoned man of God he truly is. Reverend Wright was calm and forthright. His total command of the King's English spoke well for him. I watched as he explained himself while imaging the aspirin being passed around at Barack's main headquarters. They must have breathed a sigh of relief when the interview was finally over because there were no gaffs or new problems exposed.

The controversy will continue, but the American people got a chance to see a long, in-depth interview with the pastor, and now they will judge Reverend Wright for themselves. As these things go, I saw it as a positive for the Obama campaign regardless of the timing. The Clinton campaign will certainly try to use something Reverend Wright said against Obama. The comeback bus needs fuel for its engine or it will run out of gas. Anything negative is fuel for the fire, and scorching the earth seems to have been productive for Hillary.

Momentum must be maintained or it will turn to its fickle nature and switch sides. Any change of momentum will end this thing almost immediately. Barack must change the momentum, and he needs to do it quickly. A strong heartfelt personalized speech against the war or about stopping the rising foreclosures would probably accomplish this. Only a strong response will slow down the drive of the Comeback Kid. Just as she bounced back after finishing third in Iowa, Hillary Clinton knows how to fight when she is down. If she pulls off Indiana or North Carolina we will revisit this amazing phenomenon.

***

Things are now happening at a rapid pace. At first, it was appearances on *Saturday Night Live,* Jay Leno and David Letterman. Now all of our candidates for the most important office in the world are on the World Wrestling shows. What happened to solutions to our many serious problems? These discussions have given way to who can defeat the current champion Randy Orton or the Undertaker; of course none of them could survive a cage match. If they are really smart, a match with The Great Khali could give them a great boost with the WWE crowd.

Last night, Barack was all over TV playing a three-on-three basketball game in Indiana. This was a smart move, even if it's more pandering for the votes of the so-called "common" people. It would have been perfect if Barack had just stumbled across some teenagers playing in Gary, just grabbed some gym shoes, and joined in. Unfortunately, I have to put this in the category of a calculated move. Still, I'd love to see senators Clinton and McCain try to match Barack's crossover dribble and moves to the hole.

Unlike in bowling, Barack is a very good basketball player and knows how to use his height. It would have been great if he had really pushed the envelope and slam dunked on the young men. I'm sure he made at least one jump shot, but his only three-point shot televised bounced off the back rim.

At least these pictures will replace the gutter balls and pitiful score he got in Pennsylvania. The fact that Barack looks a little like Indiana Pacers star Reggie Miller will not hurt him in Indiana, which loves its basketball. The Hoosier State has produced some of the greatest players of all time and one of the game's greatest coaches, Bobby Knight. Before the May 6 primary, we should see Obama handle the rock at least one more time, and I hope that next time my friend slams one down with authority.

With the polls tightening in Indiana, a display of power and vitality can be just what the doctor ordered. Now, Senator Clinton will be forced to tackle Superbowl champion Peyton Manning, and Senator McCain's people are probably trying to teach him to pop a wheelie on a skateboard. I hope Barack keeps a basketball in his limo.

On April 26 the *Indianapolis Star* and the *South Bend Tribune* have Obama with only a small lead. He was up by around eight points a few weeks ago. The polls have been pretty close lately, but they haven't been as accurate as they have in previous years.

In North Carolina, Obama still has a good lead in the polls, and it doesn't appear to be shrinking at all. This is his best news of the day, and with his basketball bump in Indiana, I am predicting he will win both states and head towards June 3 having recaptured the all-important momentum. He can then close out strong in the few remaining contests. The candidate who finishes strong will impress the super delegates.

SEVENTEEN

The Power of Change

A very loud confrontation woke me up at 3:30 in the morning. A local family was having a profanity-filled, violent argument for some reason. I have become so accustomed to this kind of occurrence that I didn't even look out of my window to investigate the commotion. After the police left, I turned on the TV, and the first two stories were about more Black on Black violence in the community.

I have concluded that the only hope left for Black people in America is an Obama victory. Even if he doesn't do anything to address our problems, just having a Black man as the president will have a positive effect on our main problem, which I describe as mental illness. My people are struggling with demons that begin in the mind. Self-destructive violence and self-hate permeate Black America. A lack of value on Black life can be traced all the way back to slavery, which is a condition we have yet to overcome.

Out of despair for our condition, we have become slaves to drugs, alcohol, and fast living. Every day I speak with young Black men who couldn't care less about living, dying or killing. My people are in serious trouble, and if Obama loses, the mental depression of an entire race of people will worsen.

In the loud voices of my neighbors, I could hear booze and drugs, bitterness and anger. When people are mad at the world, they often lash out at those who are closest to them, be it family or the kid from around the corner. My heart cried out to my neighbors last night because I knew their issues went far beyond the few dollars they were fighting over. Black people suffer from an identity crisis, and an Obama Presidency can restore our true identity and instill pride in our people once again. Right now we don't have very much to feel good about, that is why Barack is doing so well among Black voters. We need him.

His victory will show these young people that they can be somebody. It will fulfill dreams and end nightmares. The psychological effects of 400 years of slavery on Black Americans, followed by decades of enduring cruelty and racism has never been seriously studied with an eye towards solutions. Families and entire tribes who spoke the same language and shared the same culture were separated in order to guarantee disunity. The rape of Black women and castration of Black men were ways to dehumanize us, and the residual perceptions still haunt us to this very day. The lack of reparations for all the free labor Blacks provided has left us financially devastated, and recovery is nowhere in sight. The American dream is still our nightmare.

In the days of slavery, Blacks were prohibited from having an education and today are given inferior schools. Nobody seems to give a damn. Dr. King's dream has still evaded the Black community, and now we are losing our minority status to others. Affirmative action is being watered down or, like in Chicago, abused by the powers that be. Black on Black violence has become a way of life, and America must shoulder some of the blame.

Senator Barack Obama must win! If he is not our only hope, he is certainly a hope we cannot afford to lose. We are a people in need of psychological help and reparations, neither of which is coming our way anytime soon, but we can have President Barack Obama, we'll at least have some pride! An Obama victory will instill pride in a desperate people. It will bring hope to the poor, and it will inspire Black youth to stop the killing. You see, millions of lives are intricately involved with Barack's. His future is not his alone.

***

It is cold and dreary in Chicago today. The eerie chill in the air is similar to the feeling I am getting about the Obama campaign. I am not getting a good vibe at the moment. There are so many hopes and dreams riding on the outcome of this campaign. A defeat of our champion would be devastating, and once again dark clouds are looming.

Rev. Jeremiah Wright was the talk of the Sunday morning shows once again. The pastor was back on television saying things that made me wonder what is going through his mind. On television on the evening of April 27, Reverend Wright gave strong emphasis to Barack's middle name, Hussein, over and over again. Why, why, why? My inner voice kept asking. A right wing, white preacher had done something similar not too long ago; his emphasis on Barack's middle name was meant to imply that Obama is a Muslim, and therefore unelectable as president in America. Perhaps Reverend Wright wants to force America to see that neither race, nor name, nor religion should matter. But, all I know for certain is that this latest appearance by Reverend Wright isn't helpful for Obama. We will see that brief part of his speech replayed over and over again by those who want to derail Barack's campaign. With elections in the conservative states of Indiana and North Carolina just eight days away, the timing could not have been worse.

Yesterday, I watched two shows at the same time so I could grasp the tone of the experts on this election. My main program was *Meet The Press* with Tim Russert (who, too, has passed away since I began this book). Senator Obama was his guest, and as usual, Russert was fair, but tough. He questioned Barack and pressed him on a wide variety of issues, and Obama responded quite well. The only policy mistake I believe Barack made was on the federal gasoline tax. Clinton and McCain have suggested they would temporarily suspend the tax, but Barack disagreed because he feels the savings will not be passed down to the people. Even though they won't, consumers don't really care, they just want the prices to go down.

I was the original sponsor of a bill to eliminate the Illinois gas tax in the year 2000. The Republicans stole my idea, we call it bill jacking, and as they were in the majority, it became the law for a year. The oil companies kept the profits, but the prices at the pump did drop a bit. Obama should go along with the tax holiday and find another way to cut their outrageous profits, otherwise he will be portrayed as a tax and spend Democrat who is out of touch with the people. Sometimes the public can't handle the truth. And, Barack also voted for my bill while we served together in the Illinois State Senate, which the crafty McCain quickly pointed out.

McCain just about called Obama a disingenuous hypocrite, although Republicans historically run and win on a "no new taxes" pledge. Once they win, they raise taxes and call them fee enhancements or by some other name.

PHOTOS

(L.) Illinois State Senator Rickey Hendon with then Illinois State Senator Barack Obama when he was running for the U.S. Senate in 2004. (Photo by Anthony Jones) (R.) Former Illinois State Senator Denny Jacobs with son, Illinois State Senator Mike Jacobs, in front of the Old State Capitol building in Springfield, Illinois, at Obama's announcement of his candidacy for president on February 10, 2008.

(L.) Senator Rickey Hendon and a President Abraham Lincoln look-alike in Springfield on the day of Obama's announcement of his candidacy for president. (R.) Senator Rickey Hendon and Illinois State Senator Kimberly Lightford bundled in warm clothing on the day of Obama's announcement.

(L.) Indiana State Senator Earlene Rogers, Illinois State Senator Donne Trotter, Gary, Indiana Mayor Rudy Clay, and Senator Kimberly Lightford at campaign headquarters on Indiana Primary Day, May 6, 2008. (R.) Senator Kimberly Lightford and Senator Hendon on the floor of the Democratic National Convention in Denver. (Photo by Beverly Swanigan)

(L.) Clinton Delegate DelMarie Cobb with Senator Hendon at the Democratic National Convention in Denver. (Photo by Beverly Swanigan) (R.) Chicago Mayor Richard Daley with an emotional Congressman Jesse Jackson Jr. at Illinois Democrat's Unity Breakfast at the Democratic National Convention in Denver.

(L.) Senator Hendon with His Excellency Prince Asiel Ben Israel and Senator Donne Trotter at the Democratic National Convention in Denver. (Photo by Yesse Yehudah) (R.) Senator Hendon with Chicago radio personality Cliff Kelley. (Photos by Beverly Swanigan)

(L.) Former Illinois State Senator and Clinton Delegate, Alice Palmer, former Illinois Comptroller Roland Burris and DelMarie Cobb at the Democratic National Convention in Denver. (R.) Senator Hendon and Congressman Debbie Halverson on the convention floor. (Photos by Beverly Swanigan)

(L.) Senator Hendon, Illinois State Senate President Emil Jones, Senator Mattie Hunter. (R.) Illinois State Senator Kwame Raoul (who took over Obama's State Senate seat), Senator Kimberly Lightford and Senate President Emil Jones at the Denver Convention Center. (Photos by Beverly Swanigan)

(L.) U.S. Senator Edward Kennedy addressed the convention on August 25, 2008 after having arrived at the convention center in an ambulance. (C.) Former Illinois Senator Alice Palmer, who was knocked off the ballot to during Obama's first campaign for office. (Photos by Beverly Swanigan) (R.) Michelle Obama speaks as Mayor Richard Daley looks on. (Photo by Yesse Yehudah)

(L.) Congressman Jesse Jackson Jr. speaks. (R.) Commissioner Joe Berrios, Alderman Walter Burnett, Illinois State Representative Monique Davis, Senator Kimberly Lightford, and Senator Rickey Hendon at the Denver Convention Center. (Photos by Beverly Swanigan)

(L.) Speaker Michael Madigan of the Illinois House of Legislators, Congressman Danny Davis and Mayor Richard Daley at Invesco Field in Denver. (R.) Barack Obama makes history as he accepts the Democratic nomination for President of the United States on August 27, 2008. (Photos by Beverly Swanigan)

(L.) Michelle Obama at Mayor Daley's reception for the Illinois Delegation in Denver. (C.) Barack Obama at Obama's headquarters at the Marriott Hotel, Illinois headquarters at the Denver Convention Center. (R.) Rev. James Lowery, former president of Dr. Martin Luther King's organization, SCLC, and Martin Luther King III at the Denver convention. (Photos by Beverly Swanigan)

(L.) Judge Greg Mathis with Rev. Jesse Jackson at the convention. (R.) Caroline Kennedy Schlossberg introduces her uncle, Senator Ted Kennedy on August 25, 2008. (Photos by Beverly Swanigan)

EIGHTEEN

A Bonanza Parallel

While I was watching my Sunday morning talk shows, the question of race surfaced once again. Various pundits have danced lightly around this issue, and, of course, Barack was forced to give that magnificent speech on the subject of race a month ago. An old episode of the western *Bonanza* gave me my opportunity today. I just happened to turn on the television during my lunch break and there it was—racism!

A great opera singer was invited to perform in town. He reminded me of Barack because his dilemmas were similar, and I'm sad to say, all too familiar. His host, who sent for him, did not know he was Black, and once the opera star got off the stagecoach, she decided to try to cancel the concert.

The great singer was stuck in town, so he attempted to get a room at the hotel, but all of a sudden it was sold out—then he watched in disgust as a white traveler behind him got wonderful accommodations. The singer tried to buy breakfast at a different place, but was told all of the food was gone. (This happened to me, too, a few years ago.) They wouldn't even give the uppity darkie a stinking glass of water. This final insult led to him punching the bartender, which causes Hoss Cartwright to have to save his life. Thank God for the good white people in America, for they offset the racists and bigots, often at their own peril.

After finding out that the opera star had performed for the Queen of England, his host put the concert back on. The singer got food and shelter from the only Black family in town. But the next day a telegram came that a runaway slave of similar build to the opera singer had escaped. The racists quickly claimed that the singer was the runaway slave and formed a lynch mob. They attacked the Black family who gave the singer food and shelter, but the Cartwrights gave the man refuge on their ranch, the Ponderosa.

Just like the white people who are helping Barack, or are friends with Barack, the Cartwrights came under attack. They were threatened with punishment. Ben Cartwright tried to prove the opera star's identity by simply having him sing a song, but even the enlightened and fair-minded sheriff said no, because, in his words—"all of them can sing!" No we cannot. And we do not all look alike, either. Barack Obama looks nothing like Rev. Jeremiah Wright, and he is not trying to be like him, either.

The world-famous singer was put in jail. Finally, word came that the runaway slave had escaped to Canada and the singer was let go. Many of the townspeople were surprised that now he did not wish to sing for them anymore. He spoke about them in harsh terms, like Rev. Jeremiah Wright, and many other Blacks who have been hurt by ignorance and cruelty.

The singer's performance had originally been planned to raise money for a starving Indian tribe, so the show went on. They found a nice, white lady to sing in the opera singer's place, and she did the best she could, but just couldn't hit that high note. Finally, Hoss talked the opera singer into performing, and he gave the town a real treat. His deep baritone voice transcended race, and he received a standing ovation from everyone except the diehard bigots, who stormed out.

All the people involved with *Bonanza* deserve credit for addressing this issue years and years ago. I was going to conclude by saying the more things change the more they stay they same, but not this time. I am going to step out on faith. Barack will shake off all of these attempts to pigeonhole him as a Black radical. He will also survive the claims that he is an uppity elitist. I know he is hurt by the lies and negatives dumped upon him, but like the opera singer, he will go on to give this country a spectacular performance as the next President of the United States of America.

***

The battle continues, but it may come to an end if Barack can win in Indiana next Tuesday. I am taking a busload of volunteers there this weekend, May 3. Current polls show Indiana to be in a dead heat, so our little trip could make a difference. Every vote will count. The good news for Barack is the way the Democrats split the delegates. In winner take all, if you win the state, you get all of the delegates. Proportional representation began in 1988. It was pushed by Rev. Jesse Jackson, who was seeking the presidential nomination at the time. Under this system, the delegates are awarded by individual congressional districts, a fairer way to award delegates.

I couldn't help but wonder if Reverend Jackson had not forced the change, would Barack be better off. There have been 45 contests so far and he has won 31 of those. But, the community should thank Reverend Jackson no matter how the final results turn out. When the single winner is given all the delegates, it disenfranchises too many voters by giving their votes to a different candidate. It also does the party a disservice because it can give a false reading on the sentiments of the Democratic primary voters.

The splitting and rewarding of delegates should be done in a way that empowers the voters, which leads to more participation because people want to know their votes count. I also believe we should get rid of the antiquated Electoral College and elect our president by the popular vote.

***

Today, I read in the paper that Barack's advisors are now talking about a Dream Ticket, with him as the co-pilot, or vice president. It wasn't very long ago when this notion was dead and buried. It shocked me that Obama's people would even utter the words. Their candidate is in the lead and there are primaries remaining. The senator himself said he wouldn't consider any discussion of the number two slot while he is number one in the race.

Obama has gone through a few tough few weeks, but to talk about accepting the number two spot with primaries remaining could discourage his volunteers who are currently fighting for every vote. Maybe if he slips badly and is overtaken before the convention, the discussion might be appropriate, but any hints in that direction are counter productive at this time.

But one thing is for sure, if Clinton wins, she needs Obama on her ticket in order to give hope to the new voters who became active just because of him. Barack does not need Hillary nearly as much. But, for me, a Barack Obama/Hillary Clinton ticket is a sure winner in November. Even if you flip it around, I believe they will carry the day and change America. There has never been either a Black or a woman as our president or vice president. We can change all of that in one election.

Can you imagine our foreign policy approach with this team meeting with leaders from around the world? They would be in awe over our diversity and impressed by the progressive thinking of the American people. If the voters elected a ticket like this, the implications would be enormous; we would be seen in a completely different light by the entire world.

Of course, there is always the possibility that this Dream Ticket could implode and be a total disaster. If they can't get along or agree about who is on first, the next four years would be a rough ride. I currently deal with the fallout from Illinois' governor and lieutenant governor not working together well. I breathe the gridlocked air caused by the residual split between the Democratic controlled House and Senate every time I go to the State Capitol. A nightmare could be waiting us dreamers who long to have it all.

***

I do not have to write about Wright again, right? Wrong! I just heard Reverend Wright on WVON talk radio in Chicago. He was at the National Press Club, and my heart sank as soon as I heard his voice. It was not what he said; it was that he said it.

Why is he addressing the national press at this time? There is nothing he can say that will help Barack come home victorious. No matter how much truth Reverend Wright lays down, only the things deemed newsworthy will get reported, and the media thrives on controversy. I have previously defended the pastor, but enough is enough!

I do not know of any private conversations between Reverend Wright and Barack, or what Barack's white handlers may have said to Reverend Wright, but pastors are human beings. They have feelings like the rest of us, and the handlers may have rubbed him the wrong way and made him angry. The death threats against him and his family could also be pushing the pastor to defend himself. Still, regardless of the real reasons behind his actions, I'm beginning to wonder if Barack should consider whether or not he and his pastor have come to the end of their journey together.

I was so happy after Reverend Wright gave his great speech in Detroit in front of the NAACP, after his appearance with Bill Moyers when the controversy first erupted. If he had just stopped right there and let his statements stand, everything would be coming up roses. He set things straight, showed his courage and vindicated himself—all without giving Barack's enemies any more ammunition. Now Reverend Wright is back on the front page, and Barack is on page eight. Not only has he taken over the coverage, but he also will become the only thing Barack gets to talk about. The press is salivating, and I'm sure the pastor knew that would happen—so I ask again, why?

Barack is going to respond tomorrow, and not a minute too soon. The TV talk shows are having a field day, and Barack's lead in various polls is slipping. Two weeks ago the talk in Chicago was all about who was going to replace Barack in the U.S. Senate. Some people were promoting themselves, and others were panting as if Barack had already been sworn in as the president. Now they probably feel a little premature. What a difference a day makes. Barack must right the ship, and I do mean quickly.

Well, I just saw Senator Barack Obama distance himself from his pastor of more than 20 years. It was clearly a painful episode that troubled him deeply. It troubles me, and I am not a member of Trinity. I felt Barack's consternation and share his pain.

My people are now choosing sides between two Black men with great anger. Black talk radio is just exploding with very bitter callers from both sides. Most of the callers are lashing out at Reverend Wright. Some are calling him a sell out who is in cahoots with the Clintons; others are claiming he was paid off and other such nonsense. But Barack is firmly pushing away from Reverend Wright in no uncertain terms. Every station has Barack apologizing for his former pastor. America's economy hasn't looked so grim in decades, and all the media pundits are talking about is where Barack went to church.

Since Trinity has a Black liberation theology, this final move by Obama is discomforting to some Black church people. Any falling out with any Black church is troublesome in Black culture. Barack's courage, though, is further evidence that he is safe enough for white people and wise enough for all Americans.

Barack's hand was forced. He was damned if he did and damned if he didn't. This entire scenario lends itself to the underlying question of this book, is he Black enough or white enough? To become president of this country he must be both, neither hot nor cold. But, it says somewhere in the Bible that if you are lukewarm, you will be spit out and not found to be pleasant to the taste. The Good Book also tells us no one can serve two masters.

These and similar sayings relate to salvation, but not necessarily to politics in a nation divided by race. The test will be to see if Barack survives this dilemma or crumbles under its weight. So far, he has done a terrific job.

NINETEEN

Indiana, Here I Come

Yesterday, I took 50 of my best workers to the great state of Indiana. I sent 15 to Indianapolis with Alderman Ed Smith, and my crew went to the city of Gary, Indiana. We were part of a large contingent of volunteers from Illinois who traveled to our neighboring state to help Barack. The labor union SEIU had a very large group at Obama's Gary headquarters, and many churches also sent busloads of workers. I haven't seen that many workers in a very long time. The volunteers were very enthusiastic and they will have a positive impact on turnout in Indiana. The primary is a few days away.

My team joined up with the mayor of Gary, my dear friend Rudy Clay. Mayor Clay has another campaign office right down the street from Barack's. He gave Obama's camp the space in this large mall off Fifth Street for their campaign headquarters.

As usual, the Obama campaign is only concerned with the Obama campaign and is not helping the mayor's local candidates. I hate this about the big race candidates. They often do not openly support those who are supporting them. When Jesse Jackson ran for president he operated the same way. The only literature we could get from Barack's headquarters is his and none of the local candidates, so we will be working from Mayor Clay's office right next door. The mayor understands, but I still don't like it.

Even when Barack becomes president, I will challenge him if I believe he is wrong and praise him when I think he is on the right side of an issue. Right now, I am going to give him a pass, as I hope Reverend Wright does. This race is much bigger than Barack or Rickey Hendon. I still think the national campaign should support those who are giving everything they have to it.

So, we will return on Tuesday and help elect Obama and Mayor Clay's entire ticket. I am going to slip Mayor Clay's ticket to some of Obama's Chicago volunteers the first thing Tuesday morning. No matter what Obama's handlers say, it is the right thing to do. We should help those who are helping us. I don't care if they get mad at me. Mayor Clay is my friend and we can easily kill two birds with one stone.

Mayor Clay asked me to speak to his volunteers and relate my personal experiences with Barack in the Illinois Senate. It reinforced my logic behind this particular book. Many people will write books about our next president, but most of them never served with him and don't have a hands-on, first person perspective. Indiana Senator Earlean Rogers urged me on also, so I gave a rousing speech. I told the crowd about his legislation and desire to serve all the people. I received a standing ovation when I was done. We are going all out in Indiana because this victory could end Hillary Clinton's tormenting run.

I told the crowd about a previous conversation I had with the mayor and Senator Rogers back in January. They came to Chicago to help because they felt this race would be all over by the time their primary rolled around. Now, Indiana is the most important state in American politics today. If Barack wins this rust bucket state, he will have all of the momentum. He already leads in Indiana super delegates five to four. His lead in the polls has vanished, but a high turnout will push him over the top. There are 85 delegates at stake and a 51-49 victory will give Barack the bulk of the delegates and stop Hillary's surge.

Indiana is very similar to Ohio and Pennsylvania. They all are about 83 percent white and nine percent Black. They all have a median income of about $43,000 per year, and they are all swing states. Indiana rarely votes for a Democrat for president, nor do the other two states. The voters here do vote for Democrats in local elections, and this should help Barack since he is from a neighboring state. The saying "all politics is local" certainly applies in Indiana, and the bodies flooding in from Illinois will give Barack a huge volunteer advantage here.

Unemployment is very high here, and Gary is struggling to rebound from the closing of steel mills and the free trade agreements. Senator Clinton is running away from those agreements as she campaigns here. I do not believe this tactic will work because people here are really hurting. Every Indiana voter I spoke to is angry about our failing economy and high gas prices. That is one reason Clinton is pushing a gas tax holiday, a very popular concept here in the Hoosier State. My crew is gassing up before we go back to Chicago because gas is 30 cents a gallon cheaper here.

Today is May 3, 2008. Unexpectedly, I ended my night discussing politics with a Republican from Florida. My dear friend, Dean Nichols, gave one of his daughters away today. The wedding was absolutely beautiful, and the conversation was very stimulating. Uncle Jimmy is a retired Navy officer who now has a dental practice in the Sunshine State. He is supporting John McCain, but his wife is for Obama. We chatted for a while and all agreed that the economy and high gas prices might doom Uncle Jimmy's candidate.

I asked Uncle Jimmy about the news in Florida as it relates to the presidential election. It was his opinion that the delegates would eventually be counted and things weren't as bad as many pundits report. But, Uncle Jimmy was certain John McCain would defeat Obama or Clinton, no matter which won the nomination. He also believed that Clinton would give McCain a harder race in Florida.

No decision on Florida and Michigan has been reached according to the head of the DNC, Howard Dean. The Chairman of the Democratic Party expressed his concerns on TV today. He said it is best to let the process play itself out. The rules committee is set to meet in early June and make a decision on this issue. The credentials committee, which issues the IDs and floor passes, is also scheduled to meet. These two committees will determine how the two rebel states will be allowed back into the process. Both states broke the rules and scheduled their primaries earlier than the dates permitted by the national party rules. In Florida, the decision was made by Republicans, who could have been up to mischief, so why should Democratic voters be punished?

My prediction is that in Florida, Clinton would get the most delegates. Since both candidates' names were on the ballot and neither one campaigned there. The delegates will most likely be split by the amount of votes each candidate received in the primary.

Michigan is a lot trickier because Obama's name wasn't even on the ballot. In this case, I believe the party would give Clinton her proportion of delegates based closely on her percentage of the vote, and Obama would be allotted whatever is left. There has been talk of splitting the Michigan Delegates 50-50, which would not give Hillary any advantage in the delegate count. Howard Dean is in a pickle and he stressed the need for a compromise that each candidate will accept as fair. Good luck with that!

Later, I was approached by a cousin of the bride's family from New York. The cousin explained that their father was for Hillary Clinton, but quickly added that the rest of the family was for Barack Obama. I found it very interesting that Barack had strong white support in big city New York, which is Senator Clinton's base.

TWENTY

The Sunday Funnies

My regular diet of Sunday morning talk shows served heaping helpings this morning. Howard Dean was a guest, and his candidness and persona was quite entertaining. He didn't commit a single gaffe, but I couldn't help but think of the "I Have a Scream" speech he gave during his run for the White House. I thought it showed excitement and energy, but the national press used it to destroy his candidacy. Maybe it was because it didn't seem genuine and came across as gimmicky, but I am still unclear on how it became his "Dukakis Moment." Either way, his demise became a blessing for the Democratic Party. When the leaders chose him as the chairman, pundits criticized his selection and Republicans salivated, but Howard Dean has helped win races all over America. He will make sure his party does the right thing on this issue of Michigan and Florida.

There was more entertainment as station after station pressed on with the Reverend Wright mess. The obvious attempt to direct political thought blanketed the screen like a fog. Later, I laughed when *Fox News*—who else but Fox—released a poll showing Hillary Clinton with a 13 point lead over Barack in Indiana. Like the baseball commentator says, "Are you kidding me?" If Clinton wins Indiana, it will be by a razor thin margin of a point or two. It bothers me when some news outlets try to create the news instead of reporting it. Nothing is funny about getting misinformation from our trusted news outlets, but it does happen. I would like to think that, like with the weather, they sometimes just get it wrong. But because, at times, I have been set upon by the major print media here in Chicago, I know it can be for sinister, and sometimes personal and financial reasons.

I also never trust polls because they can be skewed any way those doing the poll wish. In my last race, a respected news outlet claimed I had a very weak 10-point lead over my two opponents. A few weeks later, they said poll results revealed my lead shrinking and one of my opponents closing fast. I won by almost 30 points in a romp, garnering 63 percent of the vote, just as I predicted. My margin of victory was the largest winning percentage in the Illinois Senate. After the election, the *Capitol Fax* explained how it was difficult to poll correctly in Cook County. They did give just due to my large enthusiastic field operation—which cannot be polled—as the reason for their numbers being way off. I'm not sure if it was just good press to say I was in trouble or some sinister game, but I certainly proved them wrong, and they hurt their own credibility.

This knowledge gives me hope that Barack will pull out Indiana and North Carolina tomorrow. He has a very strong field operation. I have been impressed by the youth and enthusiasm of his massive numbers of volunteers. This will not show up in any poll, but it will show up in the turnout generated by these hard-working warriors. Workers will determine the victor in Indiana, and Obama is pulling out all the stops because an Indiana victory will close things out. A loss means this nightmare will never end.

Not many people reported it, but Barack did win the Guam caucus by seven votes, and the delegates were split right down the middle; the candidates received two apiece. This tiny territory of the United States also has five additional super delegates, and three of them have declared for Obama.

I call this section "The Sunday Funnies" because it seems most of the shows really underestimate the intelligence of the American people. Once again, on every show there was the Reverend Wright controversy being paraded about. Each panel had one Black commentator, and they were all asked about Obama and the preacher, as if it were not old news. Their subsequent tie-ins gently touched on the subject of race through the Black liberation theology of Trinity. To their credit, Black commentators Clarence Page, Gwen Ifill, Willie Brown, Donna Brazile, and Roland Martin never ducked this issue. They addressed race head on without flinching or watering it down.

Fox did come up with one Black man who pretended there was no longer any racism in America. The commentator asked him if Hillary Clinton's support in some sectors had anything to do with race, and he clearly stated that this was not the case and went on to criticize Barack about Reverend Wright, and everything else he could think of. Thick skin is required in this business. I'm sure if Barack caught this show, he was perplexed to say the least.

Obama has not run a divisive campaign and he has held his fire with regards to Hillary's problems. There have been a few things he could have exploited, but he chose to take the high road. His decision was wise, prudent and the right thing to do. I really hate negative campaigning. Tearing into someone else in order to get elected is the low road as far as I'm concerned. Barack has stuck to the issues and explained his positions well. Once he shedded the early debate jitters, he was in complete command.

His campaign has done everything possible to avoid making race an issue in this election. Other people have fanned these flames to no avail. We are living in a defining moment in American history, and it feels great. This November we can turn this country around and reclaim our standing as the fairest, most intelligent country in the world, and deep down in my heart, I believe we will.

TWENTY-ONE

Good News, Bad News

First thing in the morning, my team and I will head back to Indiana, the state where both the Jackson 5 and the Ku Klux Klan were born. It is an interesting state to say the least. I really hope we carry this crucial state because it is the stopgap measure for this election. If Barack can hold on to Indiana, he is home free. Hillary Clinton must win this state because a sweep by Barack will be the knockout punch for her campaign.

Indiana is a long, vertical state, just like Illinois. There are some parts of both states where you are actually in the Deep South. This part of the state is polling strongly for Senator Clinton and former President Clinton has campaigned tirelessly for his wife in this area. He is very popular with the voters here. I have a problem understanding this about the voters in Indiana because of all of the plants and steel mills that closed here after he passed the North American Free Trade Agreement (NAFTA) which resulted in many of their jobs being shipped to Mexico. Indiana's industrial economy was devastated and the unemployment rate skyrocketed.

Nevertheless, President Clinton, who they called "Bubba" in these parts, was very effective on the stump and he may pull in Indiana for his wife. He still has the gift of gab and, unlike many Black people I talk to, I still like him. He remains a powerful force in American politics and he will be for a very long time.

My team made it to Indiana around 9 A.M. I had a taping with CNN and a press conference with the governor, so I caught up with them around noon. We stopped into Barack's office and then set up camp with Gary Mayor Rudy Clay. The office was bustling with activity and filled with volunteers. The Lake County Recorder of Deeds, Mike Brown was there. He is up for re-election and my contemporary, Indiana Senator Earlean Rogers, is also on their ticket.

Despite our best efforts, we lost Indiana. The Clintons pulled it off, but not by much. Senator Clinton won a close race by around two points. The margin may fluctuate during the night, but it looks like a narrow victory for her. There are still some uncounted votes, but Barack conceded late last night. The current percentage, with 90 percent of the votes counted, is Clinton at 51 percent to Obama's 49 percent.

Illinois State Senator Kimberly Lightford and I headed back to Chicago after things began to go south. The leaders of the local Democratic Party seemed resigned to accepting the loss, and even though their local candidates are ahead and winning, the desire to celebrate has left the room. Everyone is a little sad, so we are heading home. Defeat can be a devastating and heart wrenching experience. The Black voter turnout was fantastic, and Barack did very well with white voters, but we could not overcome what is being called the "Bubba factor"—white voters aggressively courted by former President Bill Clinton.

The good news is that Barack romped in North Carolina by a whopping 14 points. This big victory boosted his lead in the popular vote by over 200,000 and increased his pledged delegate lead. When you put it all together, it was a big night for Barack because the Indiana delegates will be split right down the middle.

The vote differential also is so small it will not affect Obama's popular vote lead. Still, I find myself depressed because we worked so very hard. However, the momentum has swung back to Barack. I watched each candidate give his or her victory speeches, and Barack finally seemed uplifted. He gave a great speech filled with the passion we have been waiting for him to recapture. He thanked the people of North Carolina and he even congratulated Hillary on her victory in Indiana.

The North Carolina results had come in before Indiana's results, and the East Coast count cast a little gloom on the Clinton crowd as they waited for her in Indianapolis. Even though she smiled and pledged to fight on, you could tell the margin of defeat in North Carolina dampened her vigor. Momentum had deserted the Comeback Kid, and no amount of bravado could change that.

Well, she fights on! Today is May 10, and it is the rainiest Mother's Day I can recall. I was out in the bad weather this morning and quickly scurried for the safety of home. I guess that is what humans do in time of trouble. I pondered this question as I tried to understand what Senator Clinton meant by some of her recent comments.

Why did she tell *USA Today* that Barack is losing ground with white voters? I'm told that *USA Today* left out the words "hard working," but who cares. This seemed to me to be an appeal to race. Her comment about the working class seems to be an attempt to support the elitist title she has attached to Barack. The Clintons have more than 10 times the personal wealth than the Obamas, and she gets away with appealing to the working class as their champion, but because of race, not reality. The reality is that both Clinton and Obama came up the rough road and made it. They both are wonderful proof of the realization of the American Dream.

Why go out this way? I cannot understand it. I am so sick of everything coming down to race. I am equally sick of race baiting and those who cleverly inject race into this campaign. To continue to suggest that white people will not vote for Barack is to completely ignore the millions who already have.

Obama has been receiving 45 to 55 percent of the total vote in most states. These states have an average Black population of around 10 percent. Where do these people think Obama's other votes are coming from? They are not coming from the other large minority group. The Latino community has only given Obama around 33 percent of its votes. White people are already voting for Obama! It is wonderful, and to ignore that fact is an attempt to change the course of history.

Senator Clinton can continue her campaign for as long as she wants. She has the right to take the fight all the way to the convention floor, and she may do just that. Anything can happen, and the delegates could run to her as their savior. But such surprise endings are the stuff of movie scripts and will not likely happen here. So, why doesn't she run a positive campaign and finish with style, up or down? This would keep the love affair Black people have with the Clintons intact. I want this for myself. I still have great love for Bill and I wish him well. I also will always admire the courage Hillary showed as she stood by her man and fought for universal health care, one of my passions.

Any appeal that asks the question of whether Barack is white enough is over the top, especially at this stage in the game. This opportunity to unite the Democratic Party could be lost if she decides it's her or nobody. I will never forget the chaos of the Democratic National Convention in Chicago in 1968. Is that what we want to see in Denver this year? A bad convention will doom the nominee regardless of which candidate wins in the end. There will be people fighting each other over the candidates, physical and verbal abuse could occur, and feelings will definitely be hurt.

There is nothing good that can come from a divisive party convention. Hopefully, this will not happen because more super delegates are coming out for Obama. He is now ahead of Hillary in the count. Barack picked up a few more today, and political guru David Axelrod told the media to expect even more delegates to pledge for Barack next week.

***

Maybe I need to stop watching the Sunday morning talk shows because they are constantly depressing me. This morning, all of the talk was about the Clintons' end game. On some of the earlier shows on Fox, the distinguished panel was totally against my Dream Ticket. Only one pundit still thought it was a good idea. Their logic was reasonable, and because I serve in politics, I know backstabbing can be a serious problem, and it does occur. In fact, I wrote a political handbook by that very title—*Backstabbers*.

The pundits felt Bill Clinton would be a major distraction in an Obama/Clinton White House. I am still not convinced of that developing, however, number two often wishes to become number one, and some can't wait the eight years. A president can only serve two terms, so if Hillary Clinton accepted the vice presidency, she could take Obama's place in a relatively short period of time. If somehow she is able to overtake Barack, he could be given the same opportunity, and something is better than nothing. The next few weeks will be decisive.

The biggest thing that happened in the next few weeks was that Hillary Clinton won West Virginia on May 13 by a large margin, receiving over 70 percent of the vote. So, the Comeback Kid rides again! How many political lives does she have? I just heard her pledge to fight on and head to Oregon and Kentucky. Have you ever had a cold that simply would not go away? I am certain the Obama campaign understands that feeling. Barack himself described this primary season as a marathon. Hillary Clinton simply will not go away.

Senator John Edwards endorsed Barack the day after Hillary won the West Virginia primary, and it might be just in the knick of time. The voters who have not totally embraced Obama are Edwards' kind of voters, and many will likely be influenced by him. The endorsement's timing is very good for Obama was well. Senator Clinton has been aggressively going after the middle-class, white voter with tremendous success. Edwards appeals to this demographic, so his endorsement could help Barack bridge that gap.

Both Senator Obama and Senator Clinton sought the support of John Edwards, and his voters may follow him and give their support to Obama. This could have a positive affect throughout the South and with white, blue-collar, working-class voters, who will be important general election, as well. Obama should also do very well in the traditional Democratic states. He should do well on the East Coast, and also the Midwest, since the economy is a strong factor there, and, of course, he will carry California.

I predict wins for Barack in the traditionally Republican West. I have watched Obama's strength in the western states with great interest and have tried to figure out his appeal. I have a theory. I played softball in South Dakota a few years ago. It was my second trip there for a national softball tournament. The people of South Dakota were the nicest people in the entire world. I didn't see any Black people at all, except those from out of town, but it didn't matter. We all had a wonderful time, except for not winning the championship, of course. I also flew to Arizona to play in the ASA National Softball tournament and found people there to be friendly and outgoing. These are John Edwards' kind of voters. These voters don't know Barack Obama very well, and hopefully, Edwards can help bridge the gap.

After Puerto Rico, the only primaries left now are Montana and South Dakota on June 3. If Puerto Rico votes like most Latinos, it will probably go to Hillary Clinton. This will make the results in these last two states even more crucial for Barack's chances.

TWENTY-TWO

Bushwhacked!

I believe Barack Obama will be our next president because destiny is on his side. President George W. Bush has injected himself into the campaign with some outrageous remarks to the Israeli Parliament. Bush implied that if Barack Obama became president, Israel would be subject to the days of Adolph Hitler and the Nazis. He implied that the situation would develop because Senator Obama is naive, weak minded, and under dangerous illusions about terrorists and international security. What a crock of horse manure! This appeal to fear was an attempt to vindicate himself and help John McCain, who followed up with his own ridiculous spin on Bush's dangerous pandering.

It was absolutely the best thing that could have happened for Obama. He was quick and sharp in his response to the president. He entered into a debate that made him look very much like Bush's equal, if not more. The story is still floating around a week later. Obama has been able to completely ignore Senator Clinton and he pinned Senator McCain squarely to the very unpopular sitting president. I was so happy to hear Bush open his mouth and become McCain's Jeremiah Wright. "Keep talking GW" has got to be the sentiments in Camp Obama.

I'm advising Barack to stay after Bush all the way to the November election. I must admit, Bush has a lot of nerve. I almost puked when they reported that he was disappointed that the Saudi Arabians refused his phony request to lower gas prices. They must have shared a giggle when he made the request and offered to help them build nuclear weapon capability to offset Iran's nuclear weapon's program. Now that is dangerous and mind-boggling. Maybe that is why he went off the deep end in Israel—I'm certain they heard his nuclear comments to this Arab nation.

As usual, if Bush can get the people to worry about an outside enemy, he can distract us from his administration's failures on domestic policies. Right before Bush's last election, up popped Osama bin Laden on tape. I wouldn't be surprised at anything that happens before these November elections. I have no idea how far they will go to maintain their power. Some people will stop at nothing in order to make money and control the minds of the American people.

It's easy for President Bush to make Obama the bogeyman in some parts of the country because Barack is African American. Bush might even succeed at demonizing him in some parts of the world. But, fortunately, most of America and the world are more enlightened now, and a person's race carries far less weight than it once did. However, I'm sure we will hear from President Bush again, and I hope it is soon.

***

If Barack didn't have enough craziness coming his way, he most certainly does now. Former Arkansas governor, Mike Huckabee, just cracked a crude joke at a National Rifle Association banquet referring to a gun being pointed at Barack's head! There was a loud noise in the background, which Huckabee referred to as if it could have been a shot fired, or Barack ducking for cover. He was just on television apologizing, but the damage has been done. The man is playing with fire; he should know what the assassination of Senator Obama would do to this country.

To say something like that is to put Barack's life in grave danger. There are too many crazy people in America for a major political figure to be that reckless with another man's life. His comments may have been made to boost his chances of becoming Senator McCain's running mate by appealing to white racists, but John McCain would be foolish to choose him now, that is unless he found Huckabee's comments to be as funny as his NRA audience did.

It only takes one idiot and a momentary lapse in security for yet another tragic assassination of a Black leader to occur, and Governor Huckabee has to know this. I do not accept Mike Huckabee's weak apology. This is no laughing matter, and Huckabee couldn't have picked a worst audience—people who love to hunt and fire all kinds of weapons. Perhaps he forgot about the previous presidents and political leaders whose lives were taken from them, or the civil rights leaders who died vicious, violent deaths at the hands of assassins. Then again, maybe he remembers all too well; God only knows what he was thinking.

He could have just given the green light to some very bad people without intending to do so. Can you imagine the fire storm if Barack had said something like that? Regardless of his intentions, Huckabee has done a great disservice to our great country, and I am appalled. First, Bush brings up terrorism, Hitler, and the Nazis, as if they relate to Barack Obama, and now, Huckabee cracks jokes about the murder of the young senator. I'm beginning to feel a little nauseated about all of this manipulative, dangerous, and deadly political rhetoric. This is madness at its worst level, and it could ignite a fire in this country that would burn for decades.

Maybe the thought of having a Black president is too much for some people to stomach. They may feel that the former slave must remain in his place and this experiment with change has gone too far. In my heart, I pray that America will reject the politics of fear and race baiting, and I believe we will, but the powers that be will not let go without a serious fight.

TWENTY-THREE

The End Game

Today is May 19, 2008, and the end is finally within sight. Tomorrow, there are two very big primaries in Kentucky and Oregon, though there is not as much hype over these two races as there was in the last twin bill of Indiana and North Carolina. This could be because the dust has finally settled. A split tomorrow assures Obama the nomination. Barack is expected to win Oregon, as he has most of the West, and Hillary Clinton is expected to win a narrow victory in Kentucky. Oregon has 65 delegates and Kentucky has 60—so, a split is a big win for Obama.

It would be fitting if the race would conclude in Oregon where their football team is doing so well lately. The Oregon Ducks are one of my favorite teams. The Ducks have a great offense, and over 80,000 came out to see and hear Obama speak at their stadium yesterday. It was a spectacular crowd that included boats sailing in the waters nearby.

The Kentucky Wild Cats have a tradition of great basketball teams. They have been champions for years and are always fierce competitors. Just like the highly motivated senator from New York, they fight to the bitter end. Their epic battles against Louisville are legendary. It would be fitting for the Comeback Kid's quest for the ultimate prize to end here.

At last glance, all indications are that she will fight on until the final buzzer. I hope she will bow out gracefully tomorrow night, but I don't believe she will. Either way, the end game feels close. I'm certain Barack can feel the comforting presence of the finish line as the clock ticks down and the lead is in hand. In fact, tomorrow night, after the polls close and the votes have been counted, Barack will celebrate securing the majority of the pledged delegates in Iowa, where it all began.

That is, unless something crazy happens and Oregon goes to Clinton. All of the polls indicate that this will not happen. I have wondered about Barack's popularity in the West and I've come to the conclusion that this area of our country is much more enlightened than other parts of America. Maybe the fresh air and desire to live free is the behind this refreshing phenomenon. Oregon will continue the strong trend for Obama, and the traditionally Republican West could go Democratic and carry Obama to the White House.

I actually thought the campaigns had returned to normal—vicious and devoid of truth, but normal. I was in for a big surprise. Governor Huckabee had apologized for his crude comments about Barack ducking from an assassin's bullet, and along comes Hillary Clinton with an even sadder statement. She raised the possibility that someone could kill front-runner Obama, like Bobby Kennedy was assassinated 1968, to a South Dakota newspaper. Her exact quote to the *Sioux Falls Argus Leader* was: "My husband did not wrap up the nomination in 1992 until he won the California primary somewhere in the middle of June, right? We all remember Bobby Kennedy was assassinated in June in California. You know, I just, I just don't understand."

She was explaining that she should not get out of the race because Barack could get killed before securing the nomination. This is an outrage that no apology in the world can take back or clean up what she inferred. I am totally disgusted with Hillary Clinton and my heart has been broken. She was once a true hero to Blacks in America, and now her legacy is doomed forever.

I listened to Black talk radio on my way back from the capitol, and the callers were outraged. There is a thin line between love and hate, and their love for Hillary has lunged across it. The callers read her statements to mean the exact same thing as I did. How sad. I mean, this is really awful and it could seriously damage the Democrats. If people skip voting for the top office in America, they might take a pass on voting in the elections entirely. If Clinton wins the nomination, she will lose a lot of traditionally Democratic votes in the general election. Many Black voters will not vote for her now; they are too upset.

Naturally, this will have a negative effect on the rest of the candidates in the Democratic Party. I happen to be up for re-election as a Democrat, so, of course, I'm not interested in any division or intra-party struggles for power. We need to come together, but instead, the Democrats are falling apart over this long, drawn out nomination process. The longer Senator Clinton continues her fruitless quest for the nomination, the worst things are going to get.

To bring up any assassination as it relates to the outcome of the primary process is profound! To make any mention of the terrible horror that befell the Kennedy family is even more troubling because Senator Ted Kennedy has just been diagnosed with a brain tumor. The assassination comment also reminds Black people of an era in which many of our heroes were killed, including Dr. King, Malcolm X, and Medgar Evers.

George McGovern won the Democratic nomination after Bobby Kennedy was killed and then he lost to Richard Nixon in the general election. We all remember how the Nixon Presidency resulted in Watergate, and we got stuck in the Vietnam War.

It didn't take long for the furor over Clinton's remarks to subside. I must admit, I thought the controversy would go on for more than two days, but that was about it. I hate to sound like a conspiracy theorist, but it sure went away quickly. But, I understand why Barack wants to move on. One of my friends said that he believes her camp was trying to scare him into not being so open and friendly on the campaign trail. At the very least, I'm sure he has tightened his security.

At this point, I must add a little advice to my former colleague—do not choose Hillary Clinton as your running mate because I need to be able to sleep at night. There will be far too many challenges in the Oval Office for you to be looking over your shoulder. Play it safe and choose somebody else.

I am not accusing anyone of having sinister motives towards America's next president, but I do take back my belief that Barack should choose Hillary as his vice president. I now believe it would be a bad decision, even if it means losing the election.

TWENTY-FOUR

The Pulpit Becomes Political

Another video of a man of God at Trinity Church is on You Tube. In this day and age, how can anyone expect privacy at any large gathering? This is especially true at Trinity right now. This latest sermon is by Father Michael Pfleger, the white pastor of St. Sabina, a mostly Black Catholic church on Chicago's South Side who was speaking at Trinity, and I am deeply troubled over it for several reasons. First of all, as with Reverend Wright's attention-getters, the timing does not make any sense.

After the comment by Hillary Clinton that assassination was a possibility, Barack was on a roll. The incident seemed to move more super delegates to announce their preference for him in order to get this thing over with. Since she blurted out those dangerous words, the sympathy flowed towards Obama and he picked up 14 super delegates, while Clinton picked up only one.

Didn't Father Pfleger realize that the momentum had swung back to Obama and smooth sailing would assure him the nomination? Apparently not. Father Pfleger mocked the tears shed by Senator Clinton after her third place finish in Iowa. He could have gotten away with this attempt at humor if he had stopped there, but he asked for trouble when he said Hillary felt entitled because she is white. He could have said because she was President Bill Clinton's wife, but he brought up race—a sore subject for Barack. I know Father Pfleger personally. He is a very good man and a revered Catholic priest, but he resurrected Barack's preacher problem.

I was in Springfield when this story broke. I was watching

television with Illinois State Senator Kim Lightford, and the newscasters went on to name State Senator James Meeks, who is also a pastor, as another one of Obama's radical preacher friends. Does Barack have to answer for everything any Black preacher in this country says on any given Sunday? Most of the sincere Obama supporters are going to watch what they say and choose their sermons very carefully. My friend Reverend Meeks will surely be the next misquoted pastor to come out of Obama's closet. Senator Lightford and I teased him about it, and we would have had a good laugh if the situation weren't so serious.

There is no doubt that the negative spin doctors are already going through old sermons to see what they can exploit to their advantage. This has become red meat to a media that seems to be reporting sensationalized stories in order to gain ratings. I would have never thought men of God would come under this kind of attack in America, but it just goes to show you how much times have changed.

Father Pfleger apologized for the things he said about Senator Clinton, but it still will not go away. John McCain's pastor problems only lasted for one day, but Obama's will be given life for months to come. He must be torn by his decision to leave his church home, but the attacks on his pastor had become too much of a distraction and kept him off his message and on the defense. Regretfully, I agree with Barack's decision to quit his church. I am not sure I could have done it. Spirituality is much too personal for politics. But, hopefully Barack quitting his church will bring an end to the scrutiny of every little thing that comes from the pulpit of Trinity. It also should give comfort to those who still want to know if Barack is white enough—he left his church in order to calm the false fears that he was too Black.

Someday race will no longer matter in America, but that day still eludes the greatest country in the world. America's biggest downfall is how we relate to race. We remain woefully behind the times when compared to the rest of the world. People in professional life, and especially in politics, should be judged by their skills. If not, the citizens lose.

TWENTY-FIVE

The Countdown

Senator Clinton received 68 percent of the votes in Puerto Rico, Senator Obama received a measly 32 percent. This wide percentage difference has been constant throughout the primaries where Barack has averaged around a third of the Latino vote.

Most of my colleagues want to ignore the problem between Blacks and Latinos, but I believe it is in our best interest to pay attention to it. The best way to address any problem is to first understand that there is one, and then take action to solve it. Obama's campaign has to be aware of the vote patterns and they can't be happy about it. Obama has the support of the most powerful Puerto Rican congressman in America, Luis Gutierrez of Chicago, and he still got crushed in Puerto Rico. The Obama camp must work harder to explain his platform to Latino voters or the Republicans can make gains with this growing voting block. Intervention is needed and it is needed quickly.

The Latino community has been voting heavily for Hillary over Barack since the beginning of the race, and until the primary in Puerto Rico, it appeared that the rejection of Barack's campaign was just by one segment of the Latino community. But the whipping Barack took from the Puerto Ricans, roughly 2 to 1, says to me that this rejection of Barack by Latinos is across the board. So, might Latinos support Senator McCain in the general election over Barack?

Most people think a minority would find it easy, if not intelligent, to support another minority. Both African Americans and Latinos want affirmative action and equal opportunity. Both groups support more money for education and better access to jobs. The things that should unite us would seem to outweigh those issues that divide us. Black people are much more open to immigration rights than anybody else in America. In fact, Obama was more supportive of the things Latinos fought for during the primary than Hillary Clinton. So why hasn't Obama's support been returned?

Far too many Latinos see Blacks as their competition for jobs and the crumbs that fall from the political table, like affirmative action. They seem to forget that Blacks vote for things like bilingual education and drivers licenses for undocumented residents. We don't care how people get to this country because we see everyone as immigrants except for Native Americans and the children of former slaves.

But the people who come to America are in search of the great American dream, and in most of their minds that dream is not Black. The America they see and know is historically white. They can't seem to understand the dynamics of this sea of change that is upon us, or they simply see Black advancement as being to their detriment.

If it were simply economics, Obama should be an easy choice for Latinos over John McCain, if not so easy over Clinton. Barack's platform is extremely close to the one espoused by the activists in the Latino community. John McCain's agenda is to the far right of their agenda, so Latino support of Obama should be a no-brainer—except if, to Latinos, Barack isn't white enough.

I spoke with a Hispanic friend who holds a prominent position in Illinois politics. He wanted me to know that the vast majority of Puerto Rican and Mexican Democratic elected officials were firmly behind Barack. My friend acknowledged the schism between our two minority groups and pledged to help bridge the gap.

Elections should never turn on the race of a candidate—when they do, the people will always be manipulated by politicians and those that advice them. More often than not, the behind-the-scenes consultants are the people who suggest using the race card because they are paid to produce a winner. Most of them travel from campaign to campaign and have no loyalty to any particular candidate. Most of the highly-paid consultants could care less about public policy or race relations, it's win at all cost. When they do care about policy, it's far more often to the benefit of a high-paying client than the people or the country.

After Puerto Rico, Senator Clinton won South Dakota by a wide margin, but Barack won the last contest in Montana, continuing his strong showing in the West. The Clinton campaign still vows to stay in the race and win over the uncommitted super delegates. They simply will not go away even though the contest is technically over. The results of the final two primaries should be enough to put Barack over the top, but the Comeback Kid is not deterred in the least bit.

The huge margin of victory was a bit of a surprise to me in South Dakota, but there weren't enough delegates at stake to change the overall outcome. Montana was close, but all Barack needed was a victory in the final contest so he could end on a positive note and regain the momentum. Both candidates gave forward-looking speeches and praised each other. I sincerely hope this continues, but I doubt it.

June 7, and I am feeling great. I heard Hillary Clinton is suspending her campaign and backing Barack! Of course, I would have rather she ended her campaign and released her delegates to Barack, but for now, this will do. She can still score if Barack selects her to be his running mate. In her speech she praised Senator Obama and pledged to work hard for him and the Democratic Party. I was so happy, I forgave her for anything she said or did during the primaries. The Dream Ticket can destroy any McCain combination, especially an all-white male Republican ticket.

Yes, I am once again enamored with Hillary Clinton. Bill simply has to share her with me and her 18 million admirers. I sincerely believe she would help strengthen the ticket and certainly unite the party. Serving in Illinois, I've seen the destructive nature of disunity first hand.

Some of my friends are concerned that Clinton only went halfway by not completely ending her campaign. Dick Morris claims something sinister is afoot and said, on Fox, of course, that she has people digging for dirt. If something bad comes up before the coronation, she is still an option whose delegates remain committed to her.

I don't believe Dick Morris, but this could be leverage to secure the nod for vice president. No one else has that card to play, so why not play it. I had to remind my civilian friend that Barack and Hillary met secretly the other day. Who knows what was said or agreed to? This is the friend I previously mentioned who is vehemently opposed to Obama choosing Clinton.

From a media hit point of view, if Hillary releases her delegates in late June with Barack standing by her side, it would be eureka! Timing is everything in politics. If they time things right, the Democrats will be on a roll all the way to a big victory, winning all across America to control both the House and Senate—and a tall, young Black man will become president! That's worthy of the risk of having Hillary Clinton in the West Wing.

Don't think for a minute that all of Senator Clinton's supporters want her to accept the second spot if it is offered to her. Some want her to just wait four years and run again in 2012. It is much harder for the hardworking volunteers to move on than it is for politicians.

Barack's choice of running mate will be based on politics, which is the art of compromise and the ability to get what you want accomplished. If Barack decides his best chance to change the world is to not pick Hillary Clinton for vice president, all Democrats need to forget the pass and move on. If Barack does not win, he can't change anything. If we miss this chance, we will be lost, drowning in gas, dripping in blood, and smothered to death under foreclosure notices. The crisis is real, the characters are not actors, and America's future hangs in the balance. This is our defining moment, this is America's day to impress the world, and please God, move forward beyond race and misunderstandings.

TWENTY-SIX

The Politics of Age

Are we there yet? At last, we are down to the final two candidates for president of the greatest country in the world. I am almost in tears as I write this, not for Barack, but for my ancestors who are not here to witness this moment in history. My mother and father lived at a time when this would not have been imaginable, much less possible. I am not naive enough to assume victory—after all, Barack is Black and this is still America—but winning the primary is a major step towards real freedom for Black people in this country we helped build without compensation. I can't ignore the positive impact his campaign has already had on African Americans.

I know many people in my neighborhood who are talking about changing their lives because of Barack. I talk with young Black men almost every day, and they are excited and inspired at the possibility of having a young Black president. Many young people see Obama as being from a new mindset, with views closer to their new way of thinking. Most young people don't believe the older generation can relate to them. Age is the other elephant in the living room and it is playing a key role in this election. Those of us who study politics and wish to learn from the changing tide here in America must examine it.

Politics determines so many important things in life, so it must be broken down, dissected, and understood. If people don't understand politics, they will fall for the games and the result-oriented spin put out by politicians and their handlers. It is difficult for many people to think for themselves when they are bombarded with lies, innuendo, and slick commercials made by the best producers in America. Most high paid media experts poll citizens on issues before they advise candidates on which positions to take and what to say. I'm sorry to tell the public this, but most of the things politicians say do not come from their own hearts or brains. Think tanks and pollsters determine entirely too much policy, in my opinion.

But young people seem to ignore the news and the spin that dominates the normal media outlets. They are more active online and communicate and share their thoughts through blogs, e-mails and text messages. There is plenty of spin on some of these blogs and websites, but there is also a much wider variety of voices and opinions. The use of My Space, You Tube, and other popular sites also reach younger voters. Senior citizens, who may favor McCain over Obama, are far less likely to be online and are more likely to receive their information in the more traditional fashion.

This represents an important shift in American political culture. The new, very activist voter is online, text savvy, and may be downloading information from the Web while the six o' clock news is on television. If they are like my teenagers, they may still be online after the ten o'clock news has come and gone. These young people are fueling Barack's campaign and infusing it with dedicated energy. We must ask the questions pertaining to what they want. Why are they so agitated to the point of getting involved in politics? What kind of a president do they expect Barack Obama to be? What do they expect him to do, and how quickly is he expected to do it?

Let's assume we know the things dearest to the hearts of the most regular voters, the senior citizens. They certainly want a safe and sound social security system and fair retirement plans. Seniors always express their concerns to me as they relate to health care and housing. They also read the paper and watch the evening news. The seniors lobby here in Illinois is AARP, and believe me, they are a serious force. Sometimes they are overly aggressive and don't hesitate to remind you of their voting power.

Young people don't have a long history of voting in large numbers. I was active in the 1960s when young people were very involved, but since those turbulent times, subsequent generations have shown little interest in politics. Now, suddenly, all of that has changed, and I know it is good for America.

Change is a natural thing that occurs in life. The old always passes on, and the new is brought into the world. In politics, elected officials retire or pass on. Either way, new leaders must step up to take America forward. These future leaders are cutting their teeth right now in the Obama and McCain campaigns, more so in Barack's unique and historic effort. They have motivated their peers to vote and to challenge the system. For the first time in American history, the young vote may outweigh, or at least, match senior citizen turnout. If this phenomenon continues, and is not a fluke that would quickly dissipate with an Obama defeat, the political lay of the land will shift dramatically and possibly for a very long time.

With young people's distaste for the war and rage over higher tuitions and gas prices, Democrats stand to benefit from this new voting block all across the nation. McCain will have to bear the dissatisfaction with President Bush among this group. Democrats will certainly tailor their stump speeches towards this emerging force. I am certain Republicans are watching and are seeking insight on ways to swing this voting group to their side as well.

Young voters are also more open to personal freedoms, equal opportunity, and gay rights, while many seniors oppose at least one, or even all three, of these issues. Young voters also seem to be less afraid of the world, and are therefore more open to peace talks with other nations. Obama's promise to negotiate with our adversaries has huge appeal to young, college-educated professionals. Young people are more accepting of other cultures and are not stuck in fears from the past.

Senator Obama can bridge the generation gap in this country. He is old enough to understand the realities of life and young enough to want to change some of the most unpleasant realities. His opponents have already tried to make his age an issue, as if he were a teenager. They don't mention age directly because they don't want to remind us that Senator McCain will be the oldest person to ever be elected as our president if he wins. They simply say that Obama lacks experience, ignoring the fact that some of our greatest presidents had little or no experience at this level. Presidents John F. Kennedy, Ronald Reagan, Bill Clinton, to name a few, had very little foreign policy experience.

Unfortunately, the biggest question about the Obama candidacy is not about age or experience, it is about race. Can a Black man be white enough for Americans to embrace and follow into the future? Younger voters are ready to give Obama a chance; the rest remains to be seen. America will speak shortly. The entire world, and even heaven itself, is watching.

TWENTY-SEVEN

The Race Baiting Picks Up

I bought gas yesterday and paid a whopping $4.47 per gallon for unleaded regular. I put twenty bucks in my tank, and the needle barely moved. Oil just passed $150 a barrel, and President Bush has the nerve to blame Democrats and anyone else, except himself. He is currently touring Europe and sipping tea with the Queen while we starve to death and walk to work, if we can find work. To add insult to injury, the Republicans just killed a proposal to tax the windfall profits of the big oil companies. Senator McCain joined President Bush in his opposition to the bill. McCain wouldn't have a snowball's chance in hell of winning the presidency if Obama were a white male running against him.

Now, Michelle Obama is once again under serious attack. The Republican spin doctors and lie spreaders have her as their target and have spread the lie that she—oh, my gosh!—said the word "whitey." First of all, she did not use this term in any shape, form, or fashion, but the damage has been done. The major media is now talking it up. This new, big white lie, pun intended, started on the Internet with a couple of blogs, and now it is national news. Conservative radio and TV personalities have run with it as if it were gospel. If they can get people talking about Obama's wife instead of a $5 gallon of gas, they have a chance of staying in power.

Poor Michelle, God only knows the other crazy things she has had to deal with. We probably don't hear half of what is going on behind the scenes. We know about Obama Girl and her silly, salacious song. We heard about the perverts seeking to exploit their daughters, and we've heard about some death threats, but trust me, I'm sure there is a lot more that they keep in house. Michelle is a good and decent woman who doesn't deserve this terrible treatment. I know she will make a First Lady that most Americans will be proud of—and all Americans should be proud of—because she is a class act.

I missed Michelle's appearance on *The View*, but I saw numerous excerpts from the show, and she was magnificent. Michelle handled her earlier statement about "being proud of America" with finesse. It's amazing that she still has to deal with this false interpretation of her words six months after the fact. I can't remember another candidate's spouse ever being treated in such a way. Another show mentioned that Michelle is now back to campaigning for her husband and emphasized how she left her high paying job in order to do so. They put her salary out there as a negative in order to push the line that the Obamas are rich and elitist, which is far from the truth.

I recently saw TV preacher Fredrick K.C. Price of the Crenshaw Christian Center in California, preaching about racism and its correlation to sex and interracial marriage. I was glad he did not say he was an Obama supporter because then his comments would have become part of the campaign. Pastor Price, who has an interracial congregation, held nothing back as he dealt with the most important issue of our time, race. He accurately explained how the slave masters raped Black female slaves on a regular basis, and that many purchased their female slaves based on breast size, and other physical attributes, with sex on their minds. The auctioneers would make the women turn around and stripped off their blouses in order to bring in a higher price. The old slave master kept his wife and daughters far away from the Black man while he raped Black women and fathered many Black children for more free labor.

This is America's ugly history and it still permeates today. A few years ago, I gave a Black friend and his white girlfriend a ride from Springfield, the downstate capitol of Illinois. A white sheriff followed us for a while, and finally pulled me over. He asked the young lady if she was all right or were we kidnapping her. She boldly told him that she was fine and even hugged my buddy in front of the cop.

I was driving my car with my senator plates on it, but the cop wasn't fazed at all by my position and he let us know it. After checking our licenses out for what seemed like another 30 minutes, he finally let us go with a nasty frown. He kept his hand on his gun throughout this encounter and clearly wanted to hang both of us and take the girl home to her parents. In this day and age, you would think people would be over this kind of bigotry, but from personal experiences, I know they are not.

My question is, what if Michelle were white? Maybe Barack is better off having a Black wife. People who aren't with him either way are not going to vote for him anyway, but some may hate him a little less for sticking with his "own kind." Still, there may be another element that would find Barack a bit more acceptable if Michelle was not Black. I also think she would not be getting such rough treatment by some in the media if she was not dark. She might have caught a break if she was light skinned, as fair-skin Blacks are more acceptable to some.

Pastor Price was attempting to make both white people and Black people deal with this sad issue honestly. He went on to say that many Blacks in the church still feel inferior and accept this status as legitimate, and even required, in order to maintain the proper balance, and therefore felt reluctant to support a Black candidate. This man of God quoted scripture to back up his position that God does not judge people by their race, and for us to do so is a sin. I couldn't agree more.

I just received a call from the *New York Post*. The reporter is doing a story about Barack that discussed which church he should join next. I think the Obamas should pray at home for a while, and even watch which churches they visit. Any preacher who supports Barack can be used as a problem in this crazy environment. The anti-Obama media will go back through every sermon they can find to look for controversy.

I recently read a column in the *Chicago Sun-Times* by Rev. Jesse Jackson. He wrote about how nasty the campaign is about to get—very nasty—and how the pot shots were going to be ugly, and personal. That article was followed the next day with one by Andrew Greeley, which I found to be even more disturbing. Both distinguished gentlemen predicted the worst kind of general election possible for America, one determined by prejudice and mired in racial hatred.

This is a very sad situation in which we find ourselves. The dilemma Barack finds himself in continues to percolate like an old brewery run by Al Capone—it just won't stop because the demand is too high.

A June 8, 2008, *New York Times* article, "Where Whites Draw the Line: How Black Is Black" by Marcus Mabry, offers a very insightful view of the conflict. The writer correctly states that no matter how happy Black people are about Barack, his election depends on how white people view him. They go on to say that because Barack is biracial, some whites see him as "postracial." My interpretation of the meaning of that new word is to be past race—to be Black, but not too Black, is how the writer put it. I loved the hard-hitting article and appreciated the fact that it did not dance around the issue.

Clearly, Barack had better stay away from soul food restaurants and, for God's sake, avoid being photographed eating fried chicken. And don't let anyone see Michele cleaning chitterlings because that would be a deal breaker. I'll never forget how people worried about President Jimmy Carter wanting grits and sausage for breakfast at the White House. As far as I know, Barack will not change the menu and, in fact, he has a taste for traditional upscale regular American cuisine. He is not a grievance type of Black person, and this makes him acceptable enough to white people who don't feel comfortable around the type of Blacks who throw "white guilt" at them. That's Barack. Barack will not seek reparations for slavery, nor will he force any other past sins down the throats of white people.

The story mentions Barack's other constituency, who were concerned about him being Black enough. This issue recently surfaced with Barack apologizing to two Muslim women in Detroit. The day former Vice President Al Gore endorsed Barack, the women were removed from their seats directly behind Barack as cameras rolled for the photo op. A picture is worth a thousand words, and two women clad in Muslim clothing in the background of an Obama appearance is not something his campaign wanted to let hit the media. The senator's handlers were just doing their jobs, as spin doctors are paid to do. That picture would have been sent all over the world.

The writer of the article explained that the Republican Party is going to make Barack as Black as coal if that's what it takes for them to win. If they can make him into a Muslim at the same time, they will have a very good chance of defeating him. Some friends of mine, who don't understand politics as well as they think they do, took issue with the incident. I warne d them to be patient with Barack and try to understand his dilemma. The very next week it was in the news that someone joked about having to change the name of the White House to the Black House if Obama wins. This sort of thinking is much more prevalent than we would like to believe.

Barack is also under attack for not taking public financing for the general election. Public Funding Financing gives a candidate a certain amount of money, but prohibits them from raising and spending more than that amount of money. The Obama campaign decided not to accept the public money when small, individual donations began pouring in over the Internet like manna from heaven.

Charles Gibson, of *ABC News*, posed the question in a very curious way. He asked if it was fair that Barack will have much more money than McCain, who has said he will accept the $87 million in public money. Let me say that Republicans have always raised and spent much more money than Democrats, and nobody in the media complained. Only in recent history have Democrats closed the money gap. In addition, Barack is raising his money in small denominations from a wide variety of people, many of whom have never given to any politician. Why aren't the pundits encouraging these new participants instead of trying to holler foul?

There will also be a huge amount of non-regulated Republican money spent on some of the nastiest commercials in U.S. history. Obama will need every dollar he can get to counter that.

Barack's situation continues to become more dangerous by the minute. Today is June 24, and the talk of Black radio is the disgusting blogs posted about Senator Obama. One of the nasty blogs had a picture of Barack with a noose around his neck. The caption with this racist piece of manure was "Swing State!" The lynching of Black people in this country is still a sore spot and there isn't a damn thing funny about it. Lynching was blatant murder, and the suggestion that this should happen to Barack is criminal. Unfortunately, there are people in America who would string Barack up in a flash, go to church the next day, and sleep well the same night. We must be real about these ignoramuses and prepare our country against them.

Another posting on a web sight had some Ku Klux Klan members chasing Barack with the caption made famous by Rev. Jesse Jackson when he ran for the presidency. It read, "Run, Obama, Run." I found this crap equally offensive and disturbing. Again, there is nothing funny about the KKK. It wasn't that long ago when these extremists controlled governments and used violence and terror against their fellow Americans.

As much as we would like to forget about the past and move on, we must remember what happened in this country in order to prevent its reoccurrence. Obama will not talk about the past or the threats. It is not in his best interest to discuss race as it relates to this campaign. If people ignore our terrible economy, endless wars, and global warming to concentrate on race, Barack is facing a losing battle. He is intelligent enough to know this, so I will carry this burden, and believe me, it is a heavy one.

I saw Barack on television the other day, and he appeared to be perplexed by the hatred thrown his way. I know for a fact that this is new to him. Most Black people have seen racism up close and personal, but this is all new to Barack Obama. Even when he passed the bill to address racial profiling in Illinois, he admitted that it had never happened to him. I have been targeted more times than I wish to remember.

One reason Barack is not a threat to white America is because of his life experiences. He was fortunate and smart enough to attend an Ivy League school, with its enlightened Ivy League students. His fairer skin and smooth looks may have also helped spare him some of the abuse most Black people have endured all over the world. The reality of Black life is closer to my story than it is to Barack's life. It's ironic that now that he is this/close to becoming President of the United States of America, he is finding out what it actually feels like to be Black.

As a race of people, we are still the last hired and the first fired. Even though we have fought in every war to defend America, we are still victimized and discriminated against. How can anyone say our grievances are unfounded when we are less likely to get employment (except during slavery when we had a full employment program)?

A recent survey said that Black people are turned down much more often for emergency room health care. We are much more likely to be killed by the police and less likely to receive police services when we are forced to call them. Death by gunfire has become so normal in Black America we aren't even shocked by it anymore. So, when we hear about threats to hang Barack or Mike Huckabee's joke about Barack ducking gunfire, we know the possibilities are real and the consequences are grave.

If I hear one more commentator question the reasons why Barack isn't further ahead of McCain while ignoring the obvious, I am going to scream. The answer is obvious: He is Black! I believe if Barack were any other race, he would be up 20 points. I watched my Sunday morning talk shows while they repeatedly asked each other this question: Why isn't he further ahead? What's wrong with him? Not one answer I heard even mentioned the word Black. They talked about his lack of experience and so-called failure to connect with certain voters, but they skirted around his real problem: he had an African father and he has dark skin.

The latest national polls have Barack with about a five-point lead, 50 percent to 44 percent for McCain. Third party candidates Ralph Nader and Bob Barr are splitting the rest of the vote. The good news for our nation is the fact that most of the prejudiced people are from the older generation, and pretty soon, Father Time will bring an end to a lot of this nonsense, and life will usher in a new era.

I am so encouraged by the young people who have rallied to Barack's cause. We are witnessing America's future, and it is very bright. I believe Dr. King's dream is about to come true. No matter what happens in the rest of this race, America will never be the same again. Hope is in the air, progress is around the corner, and a positive change is about to blossom in America.

TWENTY-EIGHT

Stupid Is as Stupid Does

Once again, Barack Obama has been given a helping hand by an unwitting misguided jerk. The now infamous Don Imus has stuck his foot in his mouth again. On his television show, Imus attacked the Rutgers College women's basketball team by calling them "nappy headed ho's" and suggested that they were manly and unattractive. The nasty, unnecessary, verbal beating came after the young ladies won the basketball championship last year. The controversial icon apologized—like they all do—and was removed from the air for a minute.

The young ladies should have sued him and his television station for every dime they could get, but as Barack would probably do, they just accepted his contrite apology. This turned out to be a big mistake because now, Imus is at it again. I must confess that I used to enjoy his show from time to time. I found him to be entertaining and witty. His show often provided a different look at complicated issues, and his dry humor found a place on my palate. Now, I think I was a fool to help boost his ratings. I haven't watched his show since he insulted the Black women, nor have I listened to him on the radio. But just recently, Imus was on the radio commenting on the troubles of football player Pac Man Jones. He asked about the player's race. When he was told by his sidekick that the player was African American, Imus said, "Well there you go," as if that fact alone explained the man's behavior.

Young athletes of every race get in trouble, and the suggestion by Imus that it's a Black-only problem is outrageous and very hurtful, and demonstrates how ignorance and racial hatred still exist in America.

The discussion of race and the need for tolerance and understanding is back in the news and on the front burner of the American psyche. Fair-minded white people and others who are sincerely trying to overcome past fears are surely disturbed by Imus's latest distasteful comments. Spewing hatred throughout our great country is not healthy for America or its citizens.

I'm certain the Obama campaign will not comment on this controversy, but with this incident, Don Imus, just like Reverend Wright, has given us another opportunity to take a look at our feelings about color, religion, and tolerance. The question is, how will America respond? The grievance issue has been reinforced by the wicked, dry humor of a once-respected personality. It remains a legitimate issue to those affected by the mental and spiritual harm racism causes.

America must look itself square in the eye and ask if this is the kind of country we want to be. We are at one of those great crossroads in history. We can go on to live up to the vision of the founding fathers, or we can be left behind with other backward nations. Our destiny is in our own hands, and failure is not an option. It's hard to believe, but there are some people who would rather see America fail than have a Black person as our president.

Therein we find the Obama dilemma. A recent poll found that Barack was chosen as the best person to fix our economy over John McCain by 20 points. If people just voted their own best interest on what's called pocketbook issues, Barack would be up by at least 10 points. But it just isn't that simple—because of race. Race seems to trump the economy, the war, and the growing resentment with the Republican Party and President Bush.

Another recent poll suggests that only 50 percent of Clinton's supporters have come around to Barack. The commentator saw this as good news, but I see it as real trouble down the road. The same poll found that one out of every 10 Clinton supporters plan to vote for McCain. A 10 percent defection could be the death blow for Obama. Any vote that a candidate should have received that goes to their opponent actually counts as two. Barack would be better off if these disillusioned Clinton supporters simply stayed home on Election Day.

Why are so many people who were supporting Hillary Clinton having so much trouble being team players? Only the stupid would throw out the baby with the bathwater.

***

Hillary Clinton and Barack Obama officially put their primary differences behind them and made a joint campaign appearance in Unity, New Hampshire on June 27. Their first public appearance together was soaked in symbolism. They drenched each other with the adoring accolades of two lovers determined to save their marriage from the brink of divorce, and it was beautiful, unless you were a Republican. There they stood, two former combatants holding hands, making nice-nice, and solidifying the party. They looked very much like the Unity Ticket to me. Some conservative commentators tried to put some negative spin on things, but I just didn't see it.

One claimed their body language told a different story than the glowing words they shared. Having a theater background, I also watch body language very closely, and theirs was perfect. Senator Clinton made it clear that she wanted all of her supporters to join her in supporting Barack, and he in turn called her and her husband, Bill, rock stars. Barack seemed to be very comfortable with Hillary and said the Clintons were the leaders in the Democratic Party and that we need them in order to obtain victory. I agree with him 100 percent and know he would be unbeatable if Hillary was on his ticket.

I'm not sure who Barack is going to choose as his running mate, but I am certain of one thing, it will not be a Black person. In fact, there isn't even a Black name on his long list, let alone his short list. I understand the dilemma—the mere discussion of an all-Black ticket would likely lose him the election. So, I'll stop dreaming and drop the subject, but all-white male tickets have been presented to us since the founding of this country. There also has never been a woman president or vice president either, so I sincerely hope he picks Senator Clinton and really makes history.

Other names have popped up as potential running mates for Barack, but only one other woman has the strong name recognition and excitability of Senator Clinton— Caroline Kennedy. She would also be a very good choice. Currently she is serving on Barack's search committee, but nothing prevents the committee from vetting her. Most of the Kennedy family has supported Barack from the very beginning, so this could be a match made in heaven.

Other names that have surfaced include Governor Ed Rendell of Pennsylvania and Governor Ted Strickland of Ohio, both for the strategic reason of putting their large swing states into play. Senator Evan Bayh of Indiana and Senator Jim Webb of Virginia are being considered for relatively the same reason. There's also John Edwards, whom many people like, but his showing in the primary suggests that he doesn't bring the South with him, so from a strategic point of view, he probably won't be chosen.

The other female office holders whose names I heard from an inside source include Senator Clarie McCaskill of Missouri and Governor Kathleen Sebelius of Kansas. Both of these fine women are well respected and would bring in Electoral College votes, but neither is as well known as Senator Clinton on a national level.

Senator Clinton's husband is also a great asset to Senator Obama. President Bill Clinton remains a very popular person and a superstar in Democratic circles. Therefore, I believe Barack will have a better chance of winning in November with Senator Clinton as his running mate. None of the other potential candidates can match this powerful combination of ferocious campaigners and proven vote getters. The Clintons can also attract independent and swing voters to Obama. To me, choosing Hillary Clinton is almost a no-brainer, at least we know what we are getting.

TWENTY-NINE

Moving to the Middle: The Flapjack Effect

As Barack is now the presumptive Democratic nominee, pending formal nomination and acceptance at the Democratic National Convention in Denver in August, many of my friends are getting a little nervous about our hero's latest positions on numerous issues as he gets ready to battle John McCain in the general election. Most news media people have called them serious flip-flops, or changes of positions. The Obama campaign says the candidate is simply offering clearer explanations of his long-standing positions.

I call this the flapjack, or pancake scenario. When you pour the batter into the skillet, it expands as it cooks, and makes for a crisper and tastier breakfast food. The ingredients are still the same, the batter has not changed, and you can now feed or satisfy more people. And you do have to flip a flapjack or it will never get fully cooked.

The wise thing for me to do would probably be to let that explanation be my final answer, but being Rickey Hendon, I just can't do that. Too many children are dying from gun violence in Chicago, and across America, for me to accept Barack's new position on guns. I served with Barack in the Illinois Senate and I know that as a state senator, Barack was always in favor of gun control. He continued to vote for reasonable gun control as a U.S. senator and supported the Washington D.C. gun ban, as well as Chicago's handgun ban. After becoming the Democratic front-runner, he "clarified" his position on guns and said he supports hunters, handgun enthusiasts and the right for people to have a gun in their homes to protect themselves.

From Barack's own experiences on the South Side of Chicago, he knows the devastation caused by the wild proliferation of deadly weapons in our cities and his new position is a surprising change. I honestly hope he is just catering to the right or center and doesn't mean it.

Another issue that is troubling me is Barack's new, or clarified, position on domestic spying. As I recall it in Springfield, when an expansion of eavesdropping powers in Illinois was passed by Republicans, most of us Democrats voted "no." Barack always criticized President Bush for domestic spying on U.S. citizens, but now he is saying that domestic spying is a much-needed tool to fight terrorism. This flies in the face of the Constitution. I understand that the threat of terrorism is serious, but I am not in favor of giving up our privacy because of the warped ideology of some fanatics. The minute we begin eroding the very freedoms that keep America strong, the terrorists have won.

What's next? Perhaps he will change his position on ending the war in Iraq. Some people say he already has. Barack recently said we need an orderly withdrawal with honor. I read recently that the Pentagon has scheduled to send 30,000 more troops to Iraq in 2009, which sounds like an expansion, not a withdrawal, to me. We should get out immediately, and we can do so with honor because Saddam Hussein is no longer in power. Deposing him was one of the main reasons for our invasion, wasn't it? And, of course, the non-existent weapons of mass destruction. Saddam has been tried, convicted, and hung by his neck until pronounced dead. Most of his cabinet is dead or in jail, and his sons have been killed. How many more young Americans must die before we can leave with honor?

There are two other things I need to mention which must not go unchallenged. They are Barack's adjusted positions on foreign policy, and faith-based initiatives, and his position on changing or ending affirmative action.

I believe we should have an open mind when it comes to dealing with other countries. Talking is what eventually ends most conflicts, and a strong country has nothing to fear from showing restraint. Early in his campaign Barack courageously said that it is better to talk to your enemies than to ignore them. "Bush's failed foreign policies have not made America any safer," he told the press. He repeated his position that he would meet with foreign heads of state without preconditions, which sometimes can doom negotiations before they began. After receiving criticism from his opponents he backpedaled from that position and said he would have "preparations" and lower level officials would meet first.

In an appeal for the conservative church vote, Barack modified his position and said he would continue funding Bush's faith-based initiatives when he met with major religious leaders in Chicago. Just to be clear, I have no problem with faith-based initiatives or any other church not-for-profit programs. I have also supported a person being able to protect his or her home through sensible gun ownership, but times and events have changed. For instance, the Second Amendment was written at a time when we were worried about invasion from England or France. The well-armed militia was to backup our small military.

And, when it comes to programs that help minorities, I want to remind Barack, and the world, about a great man who became the first Black mayor of the City of Chicago. Mayor Harold Washington was the change candidate for mayor and our hope for the future in 1983. When he won, he told us to not worry about certain things because we had him in command—but then he died suddenly. My point here is that Black people need to concentrate on the agenda—the plan, not the man.

All of these changes seem to be part of a campaign strategy of moving towards the middle in order to win. Like it or not, it is a normal strategy for Democratic candidates for president. But, some of Barack's expanded explanations are causing uneasiness within his strongest base. Some are getting very hard to stomach. I personally have no interest to go one step forward and two steps back and call it progress. I'm sure the McCain campaign is also watching, and the Republican gets to choose his vice presidential running mate after Barack. If Senator McCain decides to select a prominent and respected Black person like Colin Powell or Condoleezza Rice, the Black vote would no longer be a sure bet for Obama. So, it would be a mistake to just move to the middle and assume that the Black and liberal vote has no place to go.

I am beginning to get that taken for granted feeling again, and I don't like it. Barack was just on television explaining his non-flip flop on the war in Iraq. He was being called a chameleon candidate who could not be trusted, and the charge is starting to really stick. Every commentator was accusing him of changing his position, and he hasn't even made his trip to Iraq yet. His press conference seemed rushed and his message was muddied. Barack also appeared to be strained and uncertain of what to say. He attempted to reiterate his previous position, but the sharks smelled the blood in the water and they tore into him and wouldn't let go. Every station I turned to was pounding the flip-flop story into the ground. The McCain campaign pounced on the issue like it was red meat and tore Barack a new posterior. The last thing Barack needs right now is to be seen as untrustworthy.

I wanted to scream through my television at Barack—"Please, Barack, don't blow this damn thing!" I also wanted to advise him to fire whoever advised him to move to the right and run away from his core beliefs. Fire somebody tonight, maybe David Axelrod, or one of his cronies. The time to change back to your original message has come. He should also fire whoever convinced him to tone it down and become as boring as McCain. If not for the so-called flip-flops he, would actually be dull right now.

I was not there when the decision was made, but Barack's style and presentation have obviously been adjusted. There may be people in Barack's campaign who need to go. Sabotage or incompetence are possibilities, even with highly-paid staff. Whatever is happening, clearly we have gotten off track and are headed for disaster if this continues. The people have lost all trust in President Bush, so a lack of trust could turn the election towards John McCain. Senator McCain also just fired one of his top people. A shakeup could be just what the doctor ordered for Barack.

It's the Fourth of July, and the fireworks outside are matched by the bombs going off over Barack's most recent policy revisions. Very few commentators are accepting his explanation that he is not flip-flopping, and the deadly charge is having tremendous effect. Trust in President Bush is at an all-time low, so the trust is extremely important for Barack because he is so new to the national stage.

If John McCain, with his Straight Talk Express, can continue to paint Barack with this unflattering brush, he may be able to beat him in a landslide. John Kerry was never able to dislodge himself from the negative charges leveled at him, and more people knew him much better than they know Barack Obama. It is never good for a politician's opponents to be able to define who he or she is, and the window for Barack to define himself is closing rapidly.

Starbucks is closing hundreds of stores and laying off thousands of workers. American Airlines is cutting flights and laying off thousands of its employees, and gas is $4.49 per gallon in Chicago. The real estate market is down nearly 20 percent and foreclosures are at an all time high, and health care is getting harder to come by. Barack cannot blow this opportunity because the lives of so many people will be affected by an Obama loss. Barack must right his ship because we lost more of our brave, young troops in Afghanistan last month than we have any month during the seven-year war there.

The tours of 2,200 marines were just extended (which is a backdoor draft), interrupting their rights to visit home and see their families. Obama must not blow this thing because the Pentagon is preparing to send another 30,000 American troops to Iraq next year, and McCain is all for it.

Children are dying in the streets, America's once solid infrastructure is crumbling, and hundreds of thousands of jobs are being lost to overseas companies. We are in a recession, and if we don't take corrective action soon, we will slip into a depression.

There is talk that General Motors might file for bankruptcy, and the auto industry will collapse if that happens. Ford and Chrysler can't be too far behind because car sales, especially American cars, are at an all-time low. Credit is hard to get, and the price of food is making eating out a true luxury, negatively affecting the restaurant and hotel industries. Barack must regain the momentum so he can save America!

Barack said after his victory in Iowa, "Hope is what led me here today." He went on to say, "We are one nation, we are one people, and our time for change has come." He also said, "In this moment in this election we are ready to believe again!" These are very powerful words, but I am afraid that the hope he spoke of is being lost. The time for change is being squandered, and the reason to believe again is being replaced with cynicism. The change he spoke of is not the change in his policies, which we are now suffering through. With every revision in policy and move to the right in order to get to the center, he is abandoning his base and taking it for granted. Barack's move to the middle of the road could elect John McCain.

Obama needs to say what he means and mean what he says. Barack should dance with the one he came to the party with, liberals, Blacks, young people and independents. Most of these voters who put him over the top are for the things he said during the primary and are not comfortable with his current shifts. We want an end to the war, reasonable and effective gun control, equal opportunity, and less Big Brother.

Black voters are used to being taken for granted by the Democratic Party, so it's no big deal with us, but I don't believe liberals and Independents will accept his revisions as easily as Black people. I spoke with an esteemed, strong Black woman who brought up these concerns to the Obama Camp, and she told me she was told, "He (Barack) can't do anything if he doesn't win."

I mentioned this very thing earlier, but this was before the long string of revisions we've had to digest and explain to our volunteers. I personally am not surprised by Barack's latest moves, but I am surprised at how far he has gone. I also wish to warn him and his handlers that some Black people with credibility are not afraid to call him out. In fact, giving Barack a complete pass is detrimental to the African American community. We must hold his feet to the fire just as we would a white nominee. Even when he becomes the most powerful person in the world, we must challenge him if he tries to change, or end, affirmative action programs, or continue this ridiculous and costly war.

Another friend called me this morning concerned about Barack's alleged disregard for the Congressional Black Caucus and many other great civil rights leaders. I heard months ago that Black newspaper publishers made numerous complaints about access to the campaign, which fell on deaf ears. Some consultant somewhere in his camp probably believes it helps Barack to ignore Rev. Jesse Jackson and other Black leaders in the public venue, in order to attract white votes. They think this shows that he is independent and not tied down by, or to, activists of any race. But this strategy is a two-sided sword, and if the Black leaders get too frustrated and run out of patience, disaster will surely follow. The civil rights leaders I spoke to are getting close to the breaking point, but they do not want to be blamed as being the reason for his defeat.

We all know the slogan, "It's The Economy Stupid!" Well, that's exactly what this election is going to mainly be about. That's why most pundits are predicting a bumper crop year for Democrats all over America. People are angry about their dwindling personal wealth and the high prices for everything, especially gasoline. Barack will be able to ride this powerful wave all the way to the White House if he can convince the American people that he can solve the pocketbook issues.

I have a solution, and a simple explanation that the everyday Joe or Jane can understand, and Barack can keep his main campaign promise at the same time—ending the war in Iraq. The money we save from ending the war could go towards stimulating our economy. President Obama could direct some of that money towards a foreclosure relief program, and still have plenty left over for job creation and health care. He can also use some of those trillions to develop alternative energy and force down gas prices.

The Defense Department will still be strong and, in fact, a rested military would be better able to handle any new conflict our new president can't solve through a new era of brave diplomacy. I believe the American people are ready for us to solve our problems at home right now. We should put America first and let the rest of the world come after our own citizens. I'll take Birmingham over Baghdad any day, and the same goes for all the other places around the world. Internal collapse is the surest way America can fall.

Our so-called allies are spending peanuts on these two wars in Iraq and Afghanistan compared to our sacrifice. These nations are putting their economy ahead of their commitment to fight terror at home and abroad. We don't owe them anything. We certainly don't owe the Arab countries the protection of our forces when they won't do anything to bring down their skyrocketing oil costs and profits.

A large amount of war savings can go to the various states for infrastructure improvements. Building up coastlines, securing our bridges and fixing our roads create jobs. Money could be sent to all of the states with flood damage, and we can send more resources to stop the fires burning in California and build new water works to help with the droughts and save America's crops. The farms will produce more food, helping curtail those rising prices, and the food we consume will be safer, leading to fewer health problems.

Barack can sell this to the American people in his sleep because it is based on real money and it makes sense. Americans are pretty smart people. It is not lost on us that we are paying lots of money to secure other people's freedoms. We know all about spreading democracy all around the world, by force if necessary. Barack can say that and flex his muscle while looking us straight in the eye. He can join President Bush and say the surge has worked, and as a result, he can pull our troops out and use the savings to help the American people.

President Obama can then go after the price gouging big oil companies with a windfall profits tax, and then drop the federal gasoline tax proportionately. Once America is on its feet, he could look at lowering that tax even further in order to promote travel and increase Americans' spending power.

There is so much money to be saved by ending these wars and downsizing, if not closing, some of our bases overseas. We can use some of that money on an urban renewal program that brings hope to the inner cities. This bold move will reduce handgun violence and relieve our overcrowded criminal justice system. It will also ease our health care crisis by reducing our trauma center cost. It doesn't take a rocket scientist to figure this out—it only takes the will and desire of the president and some cooperation from Congress. With Democratic control of the House and the Senate, much can be accomplished in a very short period of time.

The American people are looking for someone who will make a serious attempt at solving our problems. President Obama will be given that opportunity and I believe he will not waste any time.

***

My summer has just been interrupted, and I must return to the Illinois State Capitol. The governor has called us back into special session so we can solve our budget crisis. I'm now forced to deal with the "Illinois Dilemma," hatred among Democrats. So, just because Barack's allies will control both chambers in the federal government, danger still lurks around every corner. Blind ambition and power can turn a good thing into a disaster at a moment's notice.

148

We will sit around the Capitol doing absolutely nothing while the speaker and governor exchange barbs. Our bridges will fall into further disrepair, schools will suffer, and violence will continue to claim our precious children's futures. The speaker will keep us in session until August 24 or 25, and only release us so he and his followers can attend the Democratic National Convention, so Illinois won't look so stupid to the national Democrats and the entire world. Illinois should serve as an example to all Democrats nationwide. If there is disunity, the party will lose, and so will Barack Obama. Senator Hillary Clinton must be given a major role at the convention if she is not the choice for vice president, as I think she should be. She must also be allowed to push her agenda as the senator from New York in the Obama administration.

If arrogance sets in and the Obama cabinet is not open to sharing power, Barack will be a one-term president, and we all know it takes two terms to fulfill your agenda.

"Change" will not come easy, but I know "Change" is gonna come!

THIRTY

An Exceptional Joe; An Excellent Choice

As the Democratic National Convention nears to elect Barack as the official party nominee for president, we have gone into a very dangerous period. A bail bondsman was recently arrested for threatening to assassinate Senator Obama. A subsequent search of his hotel room and home turned up a large arsenal of weapons, including a high-powered rifle. Federal authorities are taking this particular threat more seriously than the previous ones.

The closer to reality an Obama Presidency becomes, the greater the possibility of his assassination. The next few months will be filled with ramped up security and nagging anxiety for everyone who understands the high stakes involved. Some people would stoop to murder to stop the election of America's first Black president.

A writer for the *Chicago Sun-Times*, Robert Scheer, understands the insanity of it all and the possibilities we face. He wrote about the recent outbreak of war between Russia and the new nation of Georgia in the August 16 issue. Scheer points out the odd coincidence that Senator McCain's senior foreign policy advisor was recently a lobbyist for Georgia. That same person headed the Committee for the Liberation of Iraq, a group that pushed for our invasion of Iraq. They pushed the non-existent weapons of mass destruction line as a reason for our involvement, which has cost nearly 4,000 American military lives and ruined our economy. Robert Scheer admits that suggesting that the current Russia-Georgia conflict was concocted, or at the very least, was "encouraged," sounds diabolical, but he still leans in that direction, and, personally, I wouldn't be surprised if it were true.

A senior McCain advisor already suggested earlier in the year

151

that a terrorist act would help his candidate's campaign, and we all know the old trick of an October surprise being a sad part of America's political legacy. When we look at the timing of Georgia's invasion of South Ossetia, which seeks independence from Georgia, it causes great pause. Doesn't America usually support people seeking freedom and independence? At this particular moment, Barack was leaving for a brief vacation, and the war gave John McCain the stage all to himself. McCain immediately denounced the Russians for attacking the Democratic nation of Georgia, while ignoring the fact that Georgia was the initiator of the conflict and recently sought independence itself.

The fanning of the old fears of communist countries is so hypocritical of the McCain campaign, especially given the fact that the Olympic Games are currently taking place in China, a communist country, with the full participation of the United States and President Bush visiting. Could some influence peddler trying to make political gain have whispered in the ear of Georgia's president that "America would come to his defense?" It is so very sad, but it is also a real possibility that this war was planned to show that this is a dangerous world and not the time to take a chance on a young Barack Obama, who doesn't have a military background.

This, and the current wars we are involved in, may cause Barack to pick a vice presidential running mate with a military background or extensive foreign policy experience, effectively eliminating Hillary Clinton and others who had a legitimate chance at being chosen. Senator Evan Bayh of Indiana and Senator Joe Biden of Delaware are now being talked up a bit more because they fit the current bill. We will know in a few days who the choice will be, but I still prefer Senator Clinton in order to unite the Democratic party.

Senator Clinton and President Clinton will be speaking at the convention next week. Her name will also be placed into nomination, and her delegates will vote for her on the first ballot. This can be a very dangerous distraction, but if she is not getting the nod to be second on the ticket, this might be the only way to satisfy her and her supporters.

Only Barack's closest advisors really know the full story, but people pretty close to the campaign, and my own political acumen, tell me that this is the case. Senator Clinton's delegates want their moment, so Barack is going to let them have it. I can't wait to get to Denver and hear her speech. I believe that after she gets her vote from her delegates, she will move to make it unanimous for Barack Obama and push hard to unite the Democratic Party.

***

Today is August 23, 2008, and the excitement is the air. Obama has just sent text messages to millions of supporters that he has chosen Senator Joe Biden to be his running mate. In his first big decision as the Democratic nominee for the presidency, Barack Obama did not disappoint. Though many people, including myself, wanted him to select Senator Hillary Clinton as his running mate, Senator Joe Biden was an excellent choice.

Most Democratic elected officials and many Republicans are comfortable with this elder statesman who has a wealth of institutional knowledge that Senator Obama lacks and most certainly needs to strengthen his ticket. Senator Biden provides Barack with the foreign relations credentials he can use to offset the current criticism he has been getting since announcing his campaign for president. Senator Biden is a fighter with unchallengeable foreign relations experience. His choice as running mate fills the alleged inexperience gap for Barack, and it will blunt the warmonger critics who claim Barack is naive to this dangerous world we live in.

Senator Biden is Chairman of the Foreign Relations Committee, and as such he has dealt with a large number of world leaders and led the Senate on dealing with international conflicts. Senator Biden's support for the war in Iraq will also help Barack with those who might be worried about Barack's ability and desire to wage war whenever it may become necessary. Senator Biden also can be a tenacious campaigner, and even ran for president himself in 1988 and 2008. He can help deliver the electoral votes from Delaware, where he currently serves, and his home state of Pennsylvania.

The fact that Joe Biden's story includes his working-class roots from Scranton, Pennsylvania, is a big plus for Barack. His roots in small-town America can help ease any discomfort white working class voters may have about this young Black man from the big city of Chicago. And the fact that Senator Biden's son is serving in Iraq is also very attractive to military families and others concerned with our national security. Senator Biden will serve the Obama campaign well on the campaign trail.

This bold choice also sends a message to the older democratic establishment, and conservatives as well, that Barack will not force too much radical change on the country. This shows that he will work within the system and that the well-entrenched power houses within the Democratic Party have nothing to fear. Barack is a cool-headed pragmatic politician who will bring stability to our country. Senator Biden helps represent that stability.

He is also an excellent choice for the most important job the vice president has: back up the president should he become unable to perform his duties. Senator Biden is an experienced leader who can be ready to step in if, God forbid, the need should arise. And, much as I hate to bring it up, no one would be suspicious of Vice President Biden being involved if something nefarious were to happen to President Obama. Unfortunately, I don't believe the same could be said of a Vice President Clinton. I believe the Black community, and other conspiracy theorists, would cast an audacious eye towards someone in the Clinton West Wing if Barack were to be assassinated during an Obama/Clinton administration. This would make it much more difficult for the domestic disturbances that would surely occur if Barack were to be lost in an assassination to be brought under control.

Senator Biden lost his first wife and daughter in a tragic auto accident just after he won his first term as senator, leaving him a single father to his two surviving young sons. One of his sons was very ill for some time, and his struggle to balance his responsibilities as a new senator with his family responsibilities makes for a compelling story of a man with great family values and moral fortitude. The selection of this strong, mentally sound man who survived such a daunting challenge shows that Senator Obama is a competent leader with the integrity to put America's welfare before political pandering.

The Republicans are already running ads using unflattering things Biden said about Barack during the primary in which they were adversaries. That old saying, "There are no permanent friends or enemies in politics, just permanent interests," is proven true once again. A primary is a family fight, but the charges flung and the statements made during one can have residual effects. Sometimes the opposition will use words said by candidates who have come together after the primary as fodder in the general election.

The Biden camp attacked the negative ads as dirty politics and trickery, but McCain stands behind them. I am certain the ads with Barack and Hillary going at it are in the can and ready to be aired. They will be targeted at discontented Clinton supporters and women. But the idea that women will vote for McCain without regard to his platform and policy positions is absurd.

Now that Barack has picked a man for vice president, I am certain the McCain campaign will now choose a woman as the Republican running mate in order to try to pull in the female vote and to show that they are the party for change, not the Democrats. The move could be a good one, but only if the woman McCain chooses is moderate and pro-choice. The thought that women will vote for McCain even if he chooses any woman disrespects the very voters he seeks to draw.

THIRTY-ONE

Barack's Historic Acceptance at the Democratic National Convention

I knew from the moment the loud speaker announced that our plane to Denver for the Democratic National Convention had been scrapped for mechanical reasons that we were in for a rocky mountain high ride. Unfortunately, I was right. While waiting two hours for our new plane to arrive and warm up, I thought about the rocky ride Barack Obama had to deal with in order to get this far. The personal attacks, threats on his life and racial connotations he had to endure were tremendous. Some of my fellow passengers became a little restless, but we caught a break and took off just before the airport had a glitch that grounded over a hundred other planes for hours. The flight encountered turbulence, and we bounced up and down like Obama in the polls, finally landing in Denver to the turbulent bubbling over at the convention. It was Tuesday, August 26, 2008, and things were in full swing.

The delegates were nervous as hell over the roll call vote that was to take place the next day. The possibility that there would be trouble was causing much consternation, and unity was not guaranteed.

Illinois Senate President Emil Jones was in the middle of a he said-she said with a Black Clinton delegate from Illinois named Delmarie Cobb. The dispute was over whether or not he had called her an Uncle Tom, and many Clinton women were furious. There were also Obama people who were complaining that the Clinton delegates kept putting the Obama buttons given to them upon arrival in their pockets. Fortunately, Senator Clinton was scheduled to speak that night and she

157

would settle things down, or blow it all up—either way, it would come to a head and be over with.

My schedule forced me to be in Chicago the first night of the convention, but I watched a lot of it with my volunteers from our district headquarters. Many of my friends spoke the first night, and I hope they don't take this wrong, but I thought the program was slow and almost boring. I also got the feeling that each and every word was cleared by the campaign and some even written by the Obama camp. It didn't seem heartfelt. I realize a convention is supposed to have rhythm and pace and you don't want to peak too early, but thank God for Michelle Obama. Her speech that night was awesome. She did her job to perfection and introduced her beloved husband to the American people.

The stories she shared with us about Barack and her family were wonderful. They filled in all the gaps and connected the dots for undecided voters. People may have needed to know that the Obamas are not "elitist," but are just average Americans who had to struggle to make it. In fact, they both serve that American model of "get an education, study and work hard and you can make it in this great country."

Now, Michelle stands as the modern day success story that will inspire young girls all over the world to strive for the things they dream about. She now serves as a beacon of hope for everyone who wants a better life for themselves and their children. The American people got to know a bright, intelligent mom who still puts her children first and truly loves her husband. I can't wait to call her "The First Lady" because she really inspired me to endure my bumpy flight and the taxicab nightmare that was soon to follow.

I am going to get my only negative criticism of the convention out of the way. The taxi drivers were overcharging people like crazy. Most of them pretended they did not know their way around, and it was obvious when they asked if you were from out of town. But I love the city of Denver and the mayor, John Hickenlooper, and his people did a great job hosting such a large crowd of Democrats. The restaurants I visited were wonderful. Unfortunately, they blew transportation. The shuttle service left an awful lot to be desired, and getting from Invesco Field following Barack's historic speech was like pulling teeth. But the city and its people were as friendly as can be, and Denver's clean inviting streets matched the fresh western air.

There were a number of speakers who did a great job, including the Democrats' last nominee for president, Senator John Kerry. He did a very good job of attacking John McCain. He talked about the two faces of his friend and how he had compromised what he believes in—he said before having a debate with Barack Obama, John McCain needs to have a debate with himself. Kerry also blunted the war critics by introducing Barack's great uncle who served with General Patton, Charlie Payne. Uncle Payne served the duel role for Barack as the war hero from his family who also happens to be white. This was a subtle way of showing that Barack is white enough for those who need that kind of comfort. Senator Kerry was magnificent.

Senator Hillary Clinton took center stage after what seemed to be the longest day in American history. It amazed me at how worried my fellow Democrats were over her speech. Rumors flew that she was going to be disingenuous and condescending towards Barack and cause a firestorm over the roll call delegate vote scheduled for the next morning. Others fretted that she would only give a lukewarm endorsement to Senator Obama. Nothing could have been further from the truth. She was fantastic! In fact, her speech was more powerful than Senator Kennedy's, who clearly inspired the entire nation, not just the Democratic Party. Hillary was partisan, blunt and totally supportive of Obama. She did leave a small crack in her endorsement, but I believe that was to appease her delegates and to leave room for the best in show, her husband Bill, who was coming behind her the next night. Senator Clinton spoke to Obama's supporters, as well as his detractors; she also gave a message to independents and disenchanted Republicans. It was obvious to me that she wrote her own speech and these were her true feelings.

I felt a tear ease down my face as she talked about the struggles of average Americans like me. She connected with my soul when she spoke about the things women had to endure and how they, too, had to fight for the right to vote. I thought about my mother and her struggles to take care of us before she passed on, and I was overwhelmed. Fortunately for me, when I looked around, I saw that other men were crying, too, not to mention just about every woman standing on their feet in our area.

My pick for vice president put the icing on the cake when she asked her supporters, why did they do it? "Was it just for me?" she questioned them. She reminded them that it was not just about her in the most unselfish tone I have ever heard, and then she called for unity around Barack Obama. She reinforced the reasons behind my love for her and provided total vindication for me—some of my closest friends who had seriously grown to dislike her. My heart was set at ease over my views of the Comeback Kid. Now, all that was left was her roll call and her husband's speech tomorrow night. For now everyone was happy and it was party time.

The Illinois delegation had a unity breakfast on the morning of the long-awaited speech by President Bill Clinton. All of the heavy hitters in Illinois Democratic politics were present. The Illinois breakfast program was meant to show the other states that we could bury the hatchet just like we wanted the Clinton people to do. With Obama being from Illinois, it looked bad that we were so divided, so an attempt at unity was underway.

The only problems were the fact that many of us just don't like each other, and Congressman Jesse Jackson Jr. had been dropped from being the third scheduled speaker to the last. This did not sit well with him, but he rose above his disgust over the slight. Congressman Jackson explained how the other delegations were watching Illinois, and how dysfunctional we have been. He then called out various people he had problems with and began making peace. He let Congressman Bobby Rush know that he held no ill feelings towards him, and they hugged in front of the podium. After that, the crowd roared approval, which led the congressman to continue. To the amazement of the packed delegation, he then sought out an old rival, State Senator Debbie Halverson. Debbie came forward and they shared a long warm embrace. The audience was now in shock, and many people were screaming at the top of their voices.

Jackson got caught up in the moment and asked if there was anyone else he needed to makeup with or had offended over the years. Mayor Richard M. Daley stood up and hugged the congressman until tears rolled down the face of my friend Jesse Jackson Jr. The crowd was in a frenzy, and the media went absolutely bananas. People began to hug each other playfully, not realizing that the esteemed congressman was sincerely moved. It was a sight to behold. In a major coup, Congressman Jackson turned to our warring governor and Speaker of the House and encouraged them to kiss and make up, and they both rose, walked to each other and embraced. I thought I was going to die!

Some powerful elected officials—at least one on the dais—rolled their eyes at Congressman Jackson, indicating that they were not loving this love fest. I believe he sensed this and didn't press his luck. And I was so glad Jesse didn't call on them to hug anyone because we never would have found the knives. Several people expressed the opinion that the congressman was faking. Others said he only did it because he wants to replace Barack in the U.S. Senate.

But, I know real tears when I see them, and this was as real and heartfelt as it gets. As one of the National Chairs for Obama's campaign, the congressman wanted to win. He explained that disunity leads to defeat, and much too much was at stake. He went on to implore us to go hug the other states' delegations and Clinton supporters as well. If this was some well-planned act, he deserves an Oscar, and I wasted my many years in theater. I believe this was a sincere attempt to move us forward, and a moment this Democrat will never forget!

Later that day, we went to the Pepsi Center for the roll call vote of the delegates. One thousand disappointed Clinton women attempted to stage a protest, but it fizzled quickly as the vote count began. Other protesters pushing a wide variety of causes surrounded the center, but they, too, were peaceful for the most part. Police were everywhere, but they showed great restraint, and no major altercations occurred. Most of the protesters were peace activists and they seemed to know that Barack was against the war so they didn't push too hard. I believe there will be more trouble at the Republican National Convention next week because of President Bush's presence and John McCain's support for this stupid war.

Inside, the roll call began and the voting was open. Senator Obama was racking up a decent lead, but Senator Clinton was still racking up some impressive numbers. When Speaker of the House Nancy Pelosi called on the state of Illinois to cast out votes, Mayor Daley yielded to the great state of New York. After the brief formalities by the New York Democratic Party chairman, the moment I had been waiting for arrived. The floor was turned over to New York's junior senator,

Hillary Clinton. She asked for the suspension of the rules and called for an end to the role call. She then asked that the delegates all vote for Barack Obama by acclamation to be our nominee for President of the United States.

Speaker Pelosi put the question to the delegates, and everyone screamed "Aye!" There weren't any "Nays!" And Barack Obama became our official nominee, making history as the first Black presidential nominee of a major party for President of the United States.

William Jefferson Clinton has to be one of the greatest campaigners of all time. I questioned the wisdom of vice president Al Gore for not utilizing this magnificent orator during his failed run for the White House in 2000. There are many Democratic operatives who believe Al Gore lost his election because he distanced himself from President Clinton, and I am one of them.

Barack did not make the same mistake, and once President Clinton took the stage and opened his mouth to speak, we all knew why. He immediately brought us all to our feet and we practically never sat back down until one of America's greatest modern day speakers was finished and off the stage. It was electric, almost magical, at the very least, exhilarating! If it weren't for term limitations, Bill Clinton would still be President of the United States of America to this day. He remains extremely popular with the Democratic base, and his total command of the stage was on full display.

President Clinton took on Bush and McCain in no uncertain terms in a way that only he could, and he was supendous. He placed a huge protective arm around Barack Obama and reminded us that 16 years ago these same people said he was too young to be president. "Sound familiar?" he quipped. He went on to state emphatically that, "Barack Obama is ready to be president!" The former president went on to say, "The world has always been more impressed with the power of our example than the example of our power." And, "If, like me, you believe America is always a place called hope, then join Hillary, Chelsea and me, and vote for Barack Obama to be President of the United States of America."

President Clinton reminded America of the peace and broadly shared prosperity we enjoyed during his eight years in the White

House. He compared his two terms to the current mess we find ourselves in now under the Republicans, lead by George W. Bush and John McCain. He set the table for Barack's acceptance speech the next day, leaving no doubt of his total commitment to victory. The rest was to be left up to America's real first Black president, Senator Barack Obama!

I missed the shuttle to Invesco Field because I waited for my friend Commissioner Pat Horton, who had purchased every Obama tee shirt in Denver. We took a taxi to the packed stadium, and after a short, but expensive ($48) cab ride, we made it past the protestors and got in the longest line in the world. At least 80,000 people were there to hear Barack's acceptance speech. We stood in that long line, which snaked around the stadium grounds like nothing I've ever seen. After the brutal three-hour wait and intense security, we finally made it in, just in time to hear Chicago native Jennifer Hudson sing the National Anthem.

I quickly grabbed a little food from one of the V.I.P. suites and noticed that Chicago's Oprah had an elaborate V.I.P. suite, but I did not have time to stop in. I ran into Rev. Al Sharpton near the elevators, and we spoke for a moment, then I made my way to the convention floor where I briefly greeted Rev. Jesse Jackson who was listening to the mellow sounds of Stevie Wonder's performance.

Barack was about to come onstage, so I took a seat provided for me by Illinois State Senator Kimberly Lightford. By the time Barack emerged from behind the huge Roman columns, the place was absolutely euphoric! Forty-five years to the day after Dr. Martin Luther King's famous "I Have a Dream" speech, here we were, finally on the cusp of it becoming a reality. Barack Obama held our collective destinies in his hand, and this speech was the defining moment.

As soon as we saw our hero, the crowd burst into wild, uncontrollable chants of "Obama! Obama! Obama!" His name had become our battle cry, and it floated high above the football stadium, past the vast Denver mountains, across the media airwaves and up into the heavens. Hopefully, our yearnings and prayers landed on the ears of God himself. Dreams of his father, dreams of my mother, dreams of Black voices, long silenced by the passing of time, were clinging to the tall, young man now standing before us. The long nightmare of slavery, civil rights violations, denial of basic human rights, and second-class citizenship was about to be over. People began to weep even before Barack uttered a single word.

The tears quickly became contagious, as if a cleansing of some sort was taking place at that very moment. A purging of pent up frustrations and lost hope seemed to engulf many Black delegates in the packed, highly energized crowd. White people and Latinos were also overcome with emotion. Barack was theirs as well, he had transcended race and defeated the Obama dilemma. Only John McCain, or a serious lapse in security stands in Barack's way to the Oval Office.

He did not disappoint the tremendous crowd, or the 37 million viewers watching on television all across America. Throughout his speech, he encouraged us to push forward with reforms that would change America for the better. He challenged all people of conscience to join him in this great moment in history to bring about the best parts of the American dream, and to end the nightmare of discrimination, poverty, and hatred.

By the time he was finished, I was exhausted from participating in the numerous spontaneous standing ovations. No prompting was necessary during the senator's absolutely awe-inspiring speech. The audience rose to its feet again and again, and many people, including grown men, wept openly. Barack Obama had answered the underlying question posed in this book. He is the right candidate for all of the citizens of this nation regardless of race, creed, gender, or color.

During his monumental presidential run and acceptance speech at the convention on August 28, 2008, Barack Obama overcame the dilemma of proving himself worthy of America's votes and is now ready to join Kennedy, Washington, Eisenhower, and Lincoln as one of the greatest presidents in our nation's history!

THIRTY-TWO

Economic Disaster Trumps the Palin Play

I wasn't scheduled to leave Denver until Saturday, so I spent the early part of Friday morning recovering from the excitement generated from Barack's speech on Thursday night. I had a huge adrenaline rush, like many of the delegates who converged on Denver. Unfortunately, it was short lived. Most of my friends were flying out of Denver that morning, so they missed the brilliant timing of John McCain's announcement of his vice presidential choice, Sarah Palin, the little-known governor of Alaska. In the blink of an eye, she matched Barack's rock star status and stole the media spotlight from what was supposed to be Obama's biggest day of the campaign. Barack's historic acceptance speech just last night now seemed like it was weeks ago.

Clearly, the news stations all felt the same way because, with the Palin announcement, the Democratic National Convention was old news almost immediately. McCain had taken Barack's biggest news day and hijacked it with the skill of a master politician or a master thief, depending on which side you were on. The McCain campaign found a way to change the game in their pick for vice president. Naming a woman to be on the ticket was the smart political move to make. For now, the McCain camp has neutralized "the making history" card and they have snatched Barack's "Change" theme.

I had warned people close to Barack to still pick a woman, even if they couldn't live with Hillary Clinton, but they mostly shoved my suggestions aside, as if they were the disloyal utterances of a naive dreamer who didn't understand the mischief the Clintons would be up to in the White House. I took the position that Barack couldn't be undermined if he doesn't win, and America's most influential political

165

couple could assure an Obama victory. It is going to take Senator Clinton and other strong Democratic women to help bring down the spunky hockey mom, and they better get started very soon or this game could be all over. Barack and Joe Biden must also take off the kid gloves and go after her record.

McCain has attacked the media effectively when it comes to Governor Palin and forced many members of the media to go easy on his nominee and her family. The first thing most of America found out about Sarah Palin was that her 17-year-old unwed daughter was pregnant. The Republican camp knew this would come out and they used it to their advantage by saying, see the Palins are just like you folks—stuff happens to all of us. They blamed the "elitist" media for making the pregnancy an issue and cried that personal family matters should be off limits. Barack agreed. My question is, when did the Family Values and Abstinence Only crowd find teenage pregnancy okay?

True religious right wing conservatives must be a little concerned about this situation. By itself, this baby mama drama might not be enough to derail the McCain/Palin ticket, but if more of these kinds of things surface, some of their true conservative Republican base could be lost—that is, unless race trumps everything. Judging by the large amounts of money now flowing into the McCain campaign, that appears to be the case. Some people will accept, say and do anything to stop America from electing its first Black president.

The McCain campaign got a big bounce by making such a bold move. The only surprise to me was how conservative Governor Sarah Palin is. I thought the woman McCain would choose would be much more moderate and at least pro-choice. I underestimated how dire his need to appease the Republican base was. This may be Barack's saving grace because the more Governor Palin's record comes out, the more likely women will take a second look at her and find her wanting.

Most of the things I have learned about Palin's politics are not what the mainstream women I talk to are looking for in a female candidate—or any candidate for that matter. I don't believe women are not smart enough to see the Palin play for what it is, a clever political move geared to appeal to their motherly instincts and desire to see women advance. The hypocrisy is that the smooth talking governor does not share their agenda on the feminist side or the governance side of politics. Her speech at the Republican National Convention was tough. It was filled with feminist themes like breaking through the glass ceiling and being able to raise children and look good while doing it.

Media access to Governor Palin has been tightly controlled since her hard-hitting speech at the convention, while her surrogates repeatedly attack the press on her behalf. In the long run, this strategy is going to run out of time, and the media is going to regain its backbone and expose her on the issues. For instance, at the convention she claimed to be against the Alaskan bridge to nowhere, but reporters easily found lots of evidence that, while running for governor, she was all for building it.

Palin also railed against pork projects and wasteful government spending. She claimed to be a fiscal conservative, even though after the federal government killed the bridge project, she kept the money once she became the governor anyway—but why bother with minor details? Governor Palin also joined Senator McCain in beating up on the big Washington lobbyists, but when she was mayor of Wasilla, Alaska, she hired the same high-priced fellows to get money from Washington for her town of 7,500 people. The question is, how much did she pay them, and what did she do with the more than $11 million the lobbyists she hates so much brought back? The facts cannot be ignored or skewed forever, and even the best spin doctors eventually run out of lies.

The media is asking about her attempts to ban certain books as mayor of Wasilla and her attempt to fire the local librarian for refusing to go along, as well as waging a vindictive campaign against her former brother-in-law, an Alaskan state trooper. A well-respected national radio network has also claimed that a waitress reported hearing Palin say, "So, Sambo beat the bitch," referring to Obama and Clinton after the results of the Democratic primary. If this claim is substantiated, it will have a devastating negative effect on opinions of her. Not only does this statement have intolerable racial connotations, but it also demeans an outstanding woman in Hillary Clinton, whose supporters McCain/Palin are still trying to hoodwink.

This comes at the same time the McCain/Palin team are demanding an apology from Barack for saying, "You can put lipstick on a pig, but it's still a pig." They claim Barack was calling Palin a pig, but he said the expression referred to McCain's policies being the same as President Bush's.

Now that her record is creeping out, and the real media scrutiny is at her elusive door, the lipstick on the pit bull is starting to smear a little, and we will see if the exposure of her positions will be enough to bring female swing voters back to Barack Obama and the Democratic Party.

It is in the best interest of the McCain campaign to keep the electorate concentrating on things they can spin. It also benefits them if they can force the Obama campaign to tiptoe around Sarah Palin because she is a woman, and then make any attack appear to be sexist or condescending. Lipstick, teenage sex, unwed mothers, pit bulls and pigs wearing makeup might just get McCain elected. Anything that keeps people from thinking about the terrible economy and the war in Iraq benefits John McCain, who is busy running away from President Bush, who was practically left out of the Republican National Convention. I know some of McCain's strategists were very happy to see Hurricane Gustav make it possible for Bush to have other business elsewhere.

Senator McCain's vetting process, the background checking of Palin, is being questioned as being too short and flawed. It brings his competence and decision-making under scrutiny and attracts criticism. The fact that Governor Palin has no foreign policy experience—something that even First Lady Laura Bush has acknowledged—in a time of international conflict is also very troubling, especially with John McCain celebrating his 72nd birthday the very day he introduced his running mate to the world.

Sarah Palin may be a pistol-packing mama, but it would have been better for America if she at least knew something about the major players on the world stage.

In her introduction speech, she praised Senator Clinton and Geraldine Ferraro as if she really admired the two powerful Democratic women. She said, "Senator Hillary Clinton put 18 million dents in that glass ceiling; women aren't through yet. We can shatter that glass ceiling once and for all." In a further direct appeal to disenchanted Clinton female voters, she urged them to "come join our cause!" The rhetoric is top notch, pure red meat kind of stuff and I must give Karl Rove and that behind-the-scenes Bush crowd their just due. They seized an opportunity and ran with it. They want to win at all costs, and America clearly does not come first with this crowd.

The only thing that matters to the operatives behind McCain/Palin is political victory, so they can continue to police the world and sell America to China and other foreign interests for a profit. All the citizens of our beloved country need to do is follow the money trail, which does not lead back to small town America.

Barack is in an alley fight, and his nice, Ivy League, gentlemanly approach is making many of his supporters nervous. Unfortunately, he seems ill prepared for this kind of battle and these are not your usual opponents. John McCain was a prisoner of war who was tortured and starved for over six years in Vietnam, and Sarah Palin has lived through frostbiting winter days and nights that last forever. Barack must stay focused on Senator McCain and show no fear of Governor Palin. Senator Clinton would have fed Sarah Palin her lunch at every turn had she been selected as Obama's running mate, and she still might as she campaigns for the Democratic nominee in the closing days of this historic contest.

Yes, Barack still must walk a fine line when it comes to the question of whether he is white enough or Black enough, but he needs to understand that people like McCain can smell fear and they will pounce on it like sharks. It is time for Barack Obama to be bold, to man up and get busy if he wants to be the next President of the United States. But, Senator Obama will become the next President of the United States of America because of one thing—the economy. The financial disaster on Wall Street and John McCain's obvious weakness on economic issues will be the difference maker.

In addition, the hiding of Sarah Palin has become more apparent during this crisis. While Joe Biden has been addressing this issue in his run for vice president, Palin has remained eerily silent.

An AP-Yahoo poll shows that white America still has its share of bigots and suggests that if white Americans didn't have negative (read: racist) feelings toward Blacks, Barack's lead in the polls over McCain would be in the double digits and about twice what it is as we end the month of September 2008, just 40, or so, days before the November 4 general election. But even the bigots—just like everyone else in America—are being forced to "look out for number one," themselves, as they suffer under the financial results of eight years of Republican control under President Bush and senators like John McCain, who voted with Bush 90 percent of the time.

The factor of race begins to dwindle when people have to pay $4 for a gallon of gas and more for milk, eggs, butter, and bread—especially when gas is only 45 cents a gallon in Saudi Arabia, which we protect with our troops. The AP-Yahoo poll suggests that negative views of all Black people by white Democrats and independents could doom Barack. No wonder Obama is in a virtual tie with John McCain when clearly there is so much resentment against Republicans and the incumbent administration.

The poll suggests that this race factor will cost Senator Obama around six percent of the vote, more than enough to put McCain over the top if the election is close—and give us more of the same, which will ultimately destroy America's fragile economy.

The poll was conducted before the latest financial disasters—the American International Group (AIG) bailout, the Lehman Brothers implosion, and the Fannie May and Freddie Mac seizures by the Bush administration. Now with the taxpayer funded proposed $700 billion bailout of a very jittery Wall Street, the average white American is wondering, hey, what about me? Who's going to bail me out?

People of every race, creed, color, gender, religion, and orientation are on the brink of foreclosure and lost jobs because of the financial strain. It is now extremely personal to the average American, not ideological, and a drowning man can't care that much about the race of the person throwing him a lifeline. Barack has been slow but steady in his response to this economic crisis, and steady is exactly what the American economy needs right now, panic would breed disaster.

Just 10 days before the Wall Street catastrophe, McCain said "the fundamentals of the American economy are sound!" He later tried to explain that he was talking about the American worker, but how can you be a sound worker without a job? McCain's lack of basic knowledge about the economy is helping Barack Obama, and recent polls now show the Obama/Biden ticket with a lead for the first time since the introduction of the silent governor from Alaska, Sarah Palin.

THIRTY-THREE

That One!

Today is October 8, 2008, the day after the second presidential debate. I watched in awe as Barack Obama commanded the town hall meeting moderated by Tom Brokaw. All of the talk leading up to this debate was about how John McCain excels in this format and how he would dominate the discussion as a result. Well, that did not pan out. In fact Senator McCain seemed uptight and ready to explode even though he tried his best to not appear to be the "angry old man" as he did in the first debate. While he injected a little humor in the very beginning, his old personality resurfaced as the debate wore on. He finally hit his low point of the night when he turned to Senator Obama and called him "That One!"

I watched as the town hall audience was taken aback by this very mean and childish phrase, which dripped with racial overtones and disrespect. That is the moment most of the commentators talked about, and they were all very critical of McCain over the outburst. Barack was already winning the debate, but McCain referring to him in such an insulting manner sealed the deal for Obama, who remained calm and did not respond. I couldn't help but wonder what he was thinking. If it had been me, I don't know if I could have stopped myself from loudly asking, "Who the [expletive] are you calling 'That One'?"

The sympathy vote was with Barack leading up to the debate because of the "terrorist charges" launched against him by the fast-fading Sarah Palin and the death of Senator Biden's mother-in-law. The word before the debate was that McCain would build on the Palin attacks and go completely negative, but that did not occur. I believe the McCain campaign had second thoughts about attempts to tie Barack to the forty-year-old antics of Bill Ayers after they realized that the Obama campaign was not going to sit still and take it. The Obama camp pulled off the gloves and dredged up McCain being one of the "Keating Five" senators accused of corruption in 1989, which ignited a major scandal as part of the larger Savings and Loan crisis of the late 1980s and early 1990s, and his involvement in the Iran/Contra scandal, which sent Oliver North to prison.

The live audience was clearly more concerned with America's current financial crisis than anything else. The news of the day was just as bad as it has been every day for the last few months. The Dow Jones dropped another 508 points, and there were anxious feelings about the $700 billion Wall Street bail out.

The extravagance and arrogance of the Wall Street crowd was also front and center last night as news spread that one week after receiving a $85 billion government bailout, the bigwigs at the insurance giant AIG partied at a plush resort at a cost of $440,000. Senator Obama demanded that they give the money back, which generated huge approval from the American people, who were appalled at the plush spa retreat with taxpayer money. It also was big news earlier that day that the outgoing CEO of AIG received a $15 million bonus, or golden parachute, on his way out the door. In testimony before Congress it also was revealed that the executive most people blamed for AIG's demise was now a million dollar-a-month consultant for AIG.

With all of the bad economic news as a back drop, and Barack Obama speaking clearly about his plans on the economy, Senator McCain didn't stand a chance. Senator McCain's body language was quite poor, his suit was awkwardly buttoned, and he leaned on everything available, which made him appear tired. The cameras were also very unkind to him in stark contrast to the tall, handsome Barack Obama, to whom the cameras and lighting were most kind. Both men walked towards, and spoke directly to, those who gave questions from the audience, but Barack was clearly sturdier and he showed no signs of being tired. According to all of the polls, his calm demeanor reassured the American people in a time of high anxiety.

The high points for John McCain came once the debate turned to foreign affairs, and he scored a few points over Barack's statements about crossing Pakistan's borders in order to kill or capture Osama Bin Laden.

I disagree with Barack on this issue, but it serves to show that he is willing to fight and do whatever is necessary to protect America's security. It is also noteworthy that he clearly seems willing to get aggressive with a Muslim nation, which should help dispel enduring fears that he has a secret Muslim agenda. He also placed the blame for the situation on President Bush, whose administration supported Pakistan's military dictator for years, and so justified a major change in policy for the entire region. Barack then skillfully tied his plans to end the war in Iraq and concentrate on the conflict in Afghanistan, to his new policy towards Pakistan and the positive effects the change will have on our economy. Gobama!

THIRTY-FOUR

The Tanking Economy Fuels Obama's Momentum

I found myself at the gas station near my apartment in the middle of a confrontation. The "very low" price for a gallon of regular gasoline had cars on each other's bumpers, and traffic was backed up into the street. Tempers were flaring, and I was forced to calm things down. We have been hoodwinked so badly, we now see and accept $3.48 as a good price for gas. People were actually fighting to get to the pump first! When I went inside, my young Arab friend who owns the station told me he could drop the price even lower, but he didn't want to start a riot. I agreed. Sam's price was the lowest in Chicago. That week prices had dropped across the board, but the average price for unleaded regular was still slightly over four dollars a gallon.

Our economy was not responding very well to what has now become a plethora of bail outs, rescue packages, bank equity buy ins and stimulus programs. The stock market has crashed for all intents and purposes, and a serious depression is on the horizon all across the world. Suddenly the logic of having a global economy doesn't sound so good. Banks are in trouble all over the world, but things are worst here in America than it is in any other industrialized nation.

Today the markets took a sharper nosedive, even though the Federal Reserve announced the infusion of billions of dollars into our failing banking system and the awarding of another $38 billion to AIG. Perhaps the thinking that failure will continue to be rewarded has not built confidence in the investors. The fact that AIG was granted this additional money, even after they took the first $85 billion and went on a highly-criticized, lavish junket, sent a signal that the culture of excesses on Wall Street have not changed. Things have gotten so bad the clock in New York that tracks the national debt as a warning to us ran out of digits. They actually had to move a decimal point and add two more spaces.

When Bill Clinton was our president, we had a large surplus, and now, we can barely keep up with the deep hole President Bush and his Republican cohorts have put us in. As a result, Barack Obama is on the verge of blowing out John McCain in a landslide. The stock market has lost 40 percent of its value; trading and sell offs have dropped it from 14,000 points one year ago to below 8500 points, and there is no end in sight.

Because of this terrible economy I predict Barack will get over 300 electoral votes, winning Virginia, Ohio, Iowa, Colorado, New Mexico, Florida, Pennsylvania, New Hampshire, and either Indiana or Missouri. Republican nominees have traditionally carried all of these states, and President Bush won most of them in both his elections for president. The only hope for John McCain is intervention from heaven or some "outside" event of dangerous proportions, such as a new war, terrorist attack or Barack's assassination. The economy is not going to turn around in the next four weeks, and McCain knows it. This election is over unless he and his minions are able to incite a riot, or inspire some loony to commit the unthinkable—kill the competition.

The drag on the top of the ticket is not the only place where the Republican Party is feeling the heat. There are at least five U.S. Senate races where the Republican incumbents are trailing, and it looks like Democrats may pick up at least a dozen House seats currently held by Republican Congressmen.

It has been widely reported that at every McCain/Palin campaign rally they are asking two incinerating questions. The first one is, "Who is Barack Obama?" The answer from some in the volatile right wing crowd has been, "A terrorist!" The next question is, "What should we do to him?" The answer, which they subtly pretend not to hear, is, "Kill him!" This has been documented by numerous people in the media and caught on tape. If John McCain truly loved America more than he loves himself, he would have been appalled and he would have given a strong rebuke to the people who shouted out these deadly answers to their deadly questions. Instead he and Palin have injected racism and hatred into the campaign and escalated their rhetoric to a fiery pitch, putting Barack's life on the line and America's future in grave jeopardy.

If Barack Obama were to be assassinated, the entire country would go up in flames. The economy would completely collapse in the ashes, and all of us would suffer. America has survived riots before, but a calamity such as this would be much worse than anything we have ever seen because it would be politically charged and extremely emotional. Many innocent people would die and businesses would be totally destroyed. Insurance companies that are already under financial strain would not be able to pay losses, and blood would cover our streets like blankets of lava from hell. This is a very dangerous game these two politicians are playing—life and death lay in the balance.

Maybe Palin's Alaska would be spared, but no other parts of our nation would be spared from the carnage and depression that would follow Barack Obama's murder. I do not believe Senator McCain is naïve enough to not understand what could possibly happen, even if he has decided that demonizing Obama is his best route to victory.

I, personally, am not ready to be in the middle of looters and the National Guard fighting to restore order, but I know I would be out in the streets doing just that. It was 40 years ago when the West Side of Chicago burned in the riots that followed Martin Luther King's assassination. The orange glow from the fires filled the entire sky, and could be seen from clear across the city. If I have to watch the West Side of the Chicago burn down again, I don't believe I would see it recover in my lifetime. I know I would feel empathy in my heart for the rioters, and I would understand their pain as I, too, would grieve for my country and the world. I have been in this predicament before, and those of us who take to the streets to help the police and National Guard become targets for both sides.

Please, John McCain, come to your senses and stop this reckless behavior. There are too many ignorant people who will take these insults against Obama as encouragement to harm him.

THIRTY-FIVE

Posted Up!

Illinois State Senator Donne Trotter called me. In a very agitated voice he asked if I had seen the *Washington Post*. He told me I was on the front page and he e-mailed me the unflattering article. The story was about Barack's early days in Springfield and how he related to his fellow state senators in Illinois. I remember agreeing to meet the reporter for the story only after he reassured me it would not be a hatchet job on Barack. I spent two hours at lunch with the young man from Washington, and it was a very open and honest interview. I must admit I never saw it coming. I was shocked when I read the story, which made Senator Trotter and I look like the evil Black twins who mercifully taunted poor Barack from his very first day in the Illinois State Senate

This simply is not true. Barack was treated just like any other freshman or rookie, the same as I was when I arrived in the Senate just as highly opinionated as Barack did. I did taunt him when he presented his "first bill"—this is a time-honored Senate tradition. We all vote "no" and watch the freshie sweat for a minute, and then we all switch to "yes" before the roll is closed. Then we clapped for Barack, joked with him and congratulated him on the passage of his first bill. All of this was left out of the story. It seemed that the writer was on a mission and he needed the "Black Boogie Man" to show that Barack overcame envy, jealousy and had the skills to eventually win us over.

The writer was also very harsh on white senators who became friends with Barack during their friendly poker games. He described them as being uneducated dinosaurs, relics of the past, and not good poker players, asserting that Barack routinely cleaned them out. Trust me, these guys were sharks and very intelligent, and Barack lost more often than he won. I believe the writer wanted to show that Barack could get along with and understand the average white person, the middle class or even uneducated white guy—that Barack was just one of the boys, chugging down a few beers, smoking a few cigarettes, and chasing an inside straight.

I waited until today, October 10, 2008, to write about being "Posted Up" by the *Washington Post* so I could respond with a reasonable mind. I decided that the article was only doing what I am attempting to do in this book: show that Barack is white enough for white people to vote for him to be president, and Black enough to be a fair president for all, and tough enough to serve. I was used as political fodder for Barack's benefit, and since I want him to win, well, so be it. I know the story makes me look bad, but if I get to see a Black president before I die, then it is worth every misleading word. For the record, Barack only voted against my district or any of my bills once, and I never voted against one of his bills. I shared many positive stories about Barack and me, but they somehow never made it to print, I guess that's how the media works. I don't mind being the sacrificial lamb for Barack but, after he becomes president, I am still going to tell him what I think about his policies. He will need the honest opinions of those around him and not yes men. I will still be invited to, and I will certainly be celebrating at, his victory party.

THIRTY-SIX

Off With His Head!

The nasty tone of the McCain campaign continues to reverberate and drip all over this election like saliva from a mad dog on a hot summer night. As if shouts of "kill him" weren't enough, now the McCain/Palin supporters are screaming for somebody to cut off Senator Obama's head. Republican fanatics are openly calling for the murder of the Democratic nominee for President of the United States of America—and they have the nerve to call Bill Ayers a domestic terrorist! They are today's domestic terrorists because to kill anyone seeking the Office of President, let alone the front-runner, because of his race, is an insane proposition filled with unintended consequences. If a successful attempt is made on Barack Obama's life, our fragile economy will completely collapse and we will have race riots all across the country.

My point is race, creed, color or gender should not matter in this day and age. America needs to wake up and move forward like the truly great nation she purports to be. McCain and Palin should be ashamed of themselves, as they have disgraced us all by allowing these calls to kill Barack to go unchecked at their rallies.

Nothing good can come from such reckless behavior. Recently when questioned about the people at his rallies who call for physical harm to be done to Senator Obama, Senator McCain said he was proud of every person who comes to his rallies and went on to say, "You should hear some of the things Obama supporters shout out about me at their rallies." Then he compared things said about him, such as, "he's erratic" and "he's out of touch," to "off with his head!" Is he nuts, or does he think we are?

***

Thank God there are only three weeks left before the election. All of the polls show big gains for Democrats across the board. New estimates suggest a pick up of as many as eight Senate seats and 20 House seats for the Democratic Party.

The only thing falling faster than our economy is Sarah Palin's popularity. The "Trooper Gate" scandal in Alaska has caught up with the governor and her husband, Todd. The bi-partisan commission set up to investigate whether or not she abused her power to have her brother-in-law fired concluded that she is guilty and that her husband violated numerous ethics laws in the firing of the police director who would not fire the brother-in-law. The McCain campaign tried to say the investigation was just a Democratic witch hunt, but that didn't fly because the investigation was conducted by ten Republicans and only four Democrats. Palin's reformer image has been tarnished and she is now seen as a negative 8 points on the ticket instead of a big plus. Maybe this is why her campaign continues to use race and hatred as a weapon against Barack.

The G7, the group of finance ministers from seven industrialized nations, including the United States, the United Kingdom, Germany and Japan, met on October 10 to discuss the global financial crisis, but no deal was cut on a global solution to the financial mess we are in, and nationalization (every country for itself) is on the rise. Things could not be worse, and there is no end in sight. The credit crunch continues, and every time President Bush holds a press conference to calm our fears, Wall Street reacts negatively. All of this gives more momentum to Obama and Joe Biden, who has recently gone on the attack for the Democratic ticket.

There is some good news and bad news coming from the McCain campaign. The good news is Senator McCain has finally realized how the smears on Obama's character were putting the country in danger by allowing fanatics free reign. He told a volatile audience that they had no reason to be afraid of Barack Obama and that they should stop with the crazy talk (kill him, chop off his head, etc.) The bad news is his own supporters booed him soundly both times he tried to backpedal from the attacks on Obama. It's hard to put the genie back in the bottle. If Barack is murdered, the blood will be on John McCain's hands and his conscience.

THIRTY-SEVEN

The Debate Over "Joe the Plumber"

Barack Obama had better check his plumbing and I do mean quickly. Normally in political jargon a plumber is a clandestine political operator. It is not unusual for them to be involved in secret operations like the Watergate break in, or some other type of subterfuge or skullduggery. I would not be surprised to find out that "Joe the Plumber" was a political operator of some sort, or a pawn of one. It wouldn't take much to place the right person at the right place and time if you knew your target's itinerary. In this campaign the stops that will be made by Senator Obama on a given day are made available to a wide circle of people, including the press.

I do not believe that this obscure plumber named Samuel Joseph Wurzelbacher just happened to be at the same place as presidential candidate Barack Obama, with a question on the edge of his tongue that targeted how Obama's tax plan might affect small business owners. I could be wrong, but I'm in politics so I take very little at face value.

Either way, the continuous injection of "Joe the Plumber" clearly gave John McCain the upper hand during the first half of the final debate between the two nominees for President of the United States. The first 45 minutes of the third and final debate centered on Obama's tax policies as they relate to small businesses in a slowing economy.

Barack had encountered Joe as he walked through a campaign swing in Toledo, Ohio. The plumber questioned Barack about the effects his tax policy would have on him if he took over the plumbing company he worked for. Joe disagreed with Barack and claimed the company he wanted to buy was making over the exempted amount in Obama's plan, which is $250,000. Joe said his "would be" plumbing company would make around $270,000, which is suspiciously just above the threshold. He accused Barack of having a tax plan would punish small business and was close to socialism. He was smart enough, or programmed enough, to refuse to say who he was voting for, but he divulged that he believed John McCain was the one who "gets it."

Senator McCain made a big fuss over "Joe the Plumber," who sounded an awful lot to me like the fictitious "Joe Six Pack" or the "Average Joe," a close cousin of the "Hockey Mom." The plumber's dilemma dominated the first 20 minutes of the debate and it continued to resonate throughout. "Joe the Plumber" was mentioned 26 times, almost twice as much as anything else, including the failing economy. This allowed McCain to control the discussion and change the subject to Barack's tax policy rather than the economy. The other early debate issues raised by the moderator Bob Schieffer also allowed McCain to press Barack very aggressively; they were Bill Ayers and the community group ACORN—which has been accused by Republicans of voter registration fraud.

Barack defended himself, maintained his cool, and stuck to his core message without taking any of the bait placed in front of him by McCain and the moderator. Barack came close to pushing back when dealing with the question of repudiating Congressman John Lewis, whom McCain called a great hero before attacking him. Congressman Lewis came under fire for telling the truth about the incendiary shouting of "kill him" and "off with his head," referring to Barack's head, at McCain and Sarah Palin's rallies. McCain made no apologizes and almost managed a fake a tear over the negative characterizations of his campaign. Barack let him off the hook probably because he wanted to limit any discussion about the dangerous calls for his assassination.

I became concerned about the outcome of this debate as Barack continued to lay back and play defense. My feeling that he was taking too much incoming fire was shared by several of my friends. But eventually Senator McCain's age told on him and he began to tire. Barack began to shoot back a little, but McCain scored by saying "I am not George Bush. If you wanted to run against George Bush, you should have run four years ago." He clearly was ready for a nasty fight, but Barack's calm disposition forced him to calm down lest he be seen once again as "the angry old man."

Barack's closing statement was extremely powerful, and the fact that he looked straight into the camera for most of the night, and as a result, straight into the homes of the voters, served him well. Most of the pundits and focus groups agreed with me—that John McCain won the first half of the debate, but faded later. They seemed to call it a draw, but I still give the clever Republican a slight win at 51 percent to 49 percent. But the big winner was "Joe the Plumber."

The obvious loser was us, the American people. The stock market continued its roller coaster ride this week, and people wanted to hear much more about the candidates' plans to change things. After the Federal Reserves announcement that our government would infuse unlimited amounts of money into our banks to loosen up the flow of available credit, the market jumped about 978 points only to drop back down a few days later, wiping out the historic one-day gain. Nothing the Bush administration has done so far has worked to ease the fears of the business community or the American people. Projections for consumer sales for the upcoming holiday shopping season are very bleak, and some people are afraid of losing everything they have. Rumors that one, two or all three, of America's car manufacturers may file for bankruptcy are causing layoffs and putting even more stress on our struggling economy. Things do not look good.

The exploitation, or intentional repeated injection of "Joe the Plumber" by Senator McCain made sure the markets and Wall Street received very little attention in the final debate, which was supposed to have been about domestic policy. It may have saved him from an huge blow out by the Obama/Biden ticket, but McCain did not score the knockout punch he needed to win the election, or even stem the flow of undecided voters towards Barack. With the winter heating prices about to hit the cash strapped consumers, I guess somebody better fix the pipes because our economy is leaking!

The truth has quickly come out and John McCain's latest foy. "Joe the Plumber," turns out to be a complete fraud. His real name is Sam and people don't even call him "Joe." In addition, he is not even a licensed plumber, plumber's assistant or apprentice. He is in no position to buy the company he works for, and he owes the state of Ohio $1,800 in back taxes. What a crock of manure! He finally was forced to admit that he is a card carrying Republican and his intention was to set Obama up.

Now the question is, who sent him? Was he paid to do it, or just used like a sucker purposely stuck in a drainpipe in order to get business? Sam is a total sham! McCain could have called him by his real name but "Joe," "Joe Six Pack," the "Average Joe" just sounds so much better to make fools out of what his campaign clearly thinks is a gullible public. McCain told reporters that he will now be campaigning with "Joe the Plumber" but that was before his fraud sprang a leak. When questioned, Joe/Sam told reporters he also likes Sammy Davis Jr. ... huh? I guess that was just to let us know he's not a racist.

The McCain campaign has begun a new mantra about some parts of our nation not really being America. The "real America" to them is places where the McCain/Palin ticket is favored. The rest of America must wear the same "socialist" label they recently assigned to Barack behind his episode with "Joe the Phony Plumber." Sad. The beauty of America is at risk when we allow radicals who spread hatred and espouse violence to have their way. If the fringe elements are successful, may God have mercy on us all.

THIRTY-EIGHT

The Power of Powell

Today is Sunday, October 18, 2008, and Barack Obama has just picked up his most important endorsement to date. Only the endorsement of the Clintons is of equal significance as the one he received today. Former Secretary of State, General Colin Powell threw his considerable weight behind Barack Obama.

A life-long stanch Republican, Colin Powell once served our nation as President Ronald Reagan's National Security Advisor. He was able to hold on to this powerful post under the Clinton administration because he was a professional soldier who always put his country first. The fact that Ronald Reagan, the hero of the conservative right, thought so highly of General Powell has a tremendous effect on those who place national security as priority number one when it comes to selection of a Commander in Chief and their number two. They can find comfort in General Powell's decision to endorse Barack Obama, especially with General Powell saying the selection of Governor Sarah Palin as a vice presidential candidate was one of his main reasons for turning away from his friend Senator McCain, whose candidacy he had initially supported. He questioned his friend's judgment in the selection of Palin as a running mate and said she is not ready to be president and made it clear that he was uneasy over the prospect.

His assertions can only hurt Governor Palin's falling popularity. A recent Washington Post/ABC poll has her as a drag on the Republican ticket for the first time. The American people seem to agree with General Powell; 52 percent told pollsters that they are less confident in John McCain because of his selection of Sarah Palin as a running mate. Only 38 percent said they were more confident in McCain because of his selection. This comes as the governor fights off attacks over $150,000 the Republican National Committee spent on her new wardrobe from ritzy designer stores and ethical questions surrounding her travel expenses as governor of Alaska.

By contrast, the General Powell said that if called on, Senator Joe Biden—who was Barack's choice for vice-president–would be ready to lead our great nation on day one. Having the support of a Republican four-star general and former Secretary of State has girded up Senator Obama's foreign policy credibility. The timing of Powell's endorsement couldn't have been better for Barack and it may prove to be the final blow to the McCain/Palin ticket.

When combined with the support of billionaire Warren Buffet, which Barack also gained, Barack can now claim powerful endorsements in the areas of national security and the economy, the two most important issues of the day. This coup is much more significant than McCain having Joe Liberman on his side and it surely will influence the decision of independents and disillusioned Republicans—and they do exist. Senator McCain was left to rattle off the names of other great American military men who are supporting him, but none had General Colin Powell's muscle.

The Obama Campaign will certainly use the Powell endorsement in television commercials in swing states, toss up states and states with large numbers of military families. The $150 million the Obama campaign raised in the month of September alone will be more than enough to spread the good news.

As Secretary of State, General Powell's battles within the Bush administration with the unpopular Donald Rumsfield are well documented and give the general a leg up on other members of the outgoing administration. The fact that Barack followed up the Powell endorsement with the announcement that he wanted to find a place for Warren Buffett and the former Secretary of State in his administration was well received in America and abroad.

The fight is not over, but McCain is down and the referee is counting, and the senator from Arizona is not showing any signs of getting up off the political floor.

This is a big blow to McCain, who has "Joe the Plumber's" recent endorsement in contrast. He tried to downplay the Powell endorsement, but the damage to his credibility is of major significance. I predict that other major conservatives will follow Powell's lead and endorse Barack in the next two weeks.

***

Today is October 24, 2008, and the economy continues to bounce up and down like a yo-yo. Small gains are being followed by huge losses. The market fell 514 points the other day taking back most of the gains after a big rally of over 900 points a week ago. Hearings are being held on Capitol Hill in an attempt to solve the problems that led to this meltdown. The former Chairman of the Federal Reserves, Alan Greenspan, testified that he has changed his mind on regulations because of the excesses among some of the greedy and unscrupulous people on Wall Street. He called our current economic crisis a "tsunami!"

Clearly we must change our direction or else a tidal wave of layoffs and foreclosures will engulf us like nothing we've ever seen before. Worst of all, with the entire world is feeling the pain of an economic implosion. World wars have resulted from fear, isolationism and economic uncertainty.

For the good of the entire world, America needs a steady handed leader who puts diplomacy and cooperation ahead of military force and invasion.

Solving our economic dilemma will be President Obama's most immediate challenge. Barack has overcome every crisis his campaign has faced, from misunderstood preachers, to his alleged relationship with Bill Ayers, plus hidden and overt racism. I have no doubt he is the right man for this moment in history. He resolved his own double dilemma: "Is he Black enough?" Yes, he knows where he came from and is willing to do something about the problems of African Americans. "Is he white enough?" Yes, he is fair enough to look out for all races and genders in America. Barack's biracial upbringing has prepared him to answer both concerns positively and go on to do great things!

THIRTY-NINE

24 Hours to History

Tomorrow night it will all be over and I will be celebrating in Grant Park with America's first Black President. Senator Barack Obama's two-year journey started in Chicago, and it is only fitting that it end here in his hometown. The McCain campaign tried to make the planning of this huge event seem presumptuous, but no one seems to be listening. This election is all over except for President-elect Barack Obama's victory speech, which I will not miss for anything in the world. Chicago's weather is infamously unpredictable, but for Election Day it seems that God has blessed Barack Obama once again and all of the weather reports say it will be in the 70's for most of the day and it will be a clear and comfortably warm night.

Mayor Daley is preparing for over one million people to join the festivities downtown at Grant Park, and that number may be a low estimate because of the balmy weather. Parties are also being planned all over the city. I will be celebrating my re-election as well with Chicago promoter Kenny Johnson and Congressman Jesse Jackson Jr. at the Hilton hotel across the street from Grant Park, where we will wait for the president-elect to arrive. We are hoping for an early concession speech from Senator John McCain, Governor Sarah Palin, or even "Joe the Plumber—any one of them will do.

This has been a long, stressful journey, and I'm glad to have been a part of this history. I hope my chronicle of the events that led us to Chicago's Grant Park on November 4, 2008, will contribute to the dialogue that is bound to continue for years to come. It will be interesting to see if my scenarios play out. I predicted a big victory for Barack Obama, and even though some polls show John McCain closing fast, I still believe Barack will get over 300 electoral votes. I think he will also win the popular vote, which will erase any and all doubt over his victory because of the way we elect our president and vice-president.

But as we continue to move toward Election Day, the McCain campaign has gone completely negative, and the death threats against Barack have increased, but he still forges ahead without showing any regard for the daily attacks that are being showered upon him. While the economy has continued to plunge downward like Sarah Palin's popularity, there have been a few bright signs. The stock market has gone up a bit and the dips haven't been quite as drastic; but the bailouts continue and are spreading to the banks and insurance companies.

"Joe The Plumber" is the new face of the Republican Party. He is even campaigning with John McCain and talking of running for Congress or maybe even President of the United States. What a joke! The Republican Party may not recover from the debacle of this campaign for years.

But while "Joe the Plumber" and the "Terminator," California's Governor Arnold Schwarzenegger, campaigned for Senator McCain, former President Bill Clinton hit the campaign trail with Barack Obama for the first time since the Democratic National Convention. Very popular former Vice-President Al Gore also campaigned with Barack in key battleground states while John McCain received the lukewarm endorsement of our current but unpopular vice-president, Dick Cheney. Things couldn't be better for Barack and his coattails will probably help my predictions of huge Democratic gains in the House and Senate come true. Early voting seems to bear this out. I voted early for the first time in my life, and the polling place was very crowded. Almost one million people voted early in Illinois and about 25 percent of the electorate have done so throughout America—mostly to the benefit of Barack Obama.

Gas prices have finally come down, which could help Senator McCain. I paid $2.98 a gallon the other day, but Osama bin Laden has not surfaced and time for a serious October surprise is running out. It looks like the fat lady is clearing her throat!